THIS BOOK BELONGS TO

_____

START DATE

_____

SHE READS TRUTH

EXECUTIVE

FOUNDER/CHIEF EXECUTIVE OFFICER
Raechel Myers

CO-FOUNDER/CHIEF CONTENT OFFICER
Amanda Bible Williams

CHIEF OPERATING OFFICER
Ryan Myers

EXECUTIVE ASSISTANT
Sarah Andereck

EDITORIAL

EDITORIAL DIRECTOR
Jessica Lamb

CONTENT EDITOR
Kara Gause

ASSOCIATE EDITORS
Bailey Gillespie
Ellen Taylor
Tameshia Williams

EDITORIAL ASSISTANT
Hannah Little

CREATIVE

CREATIVE DIRECTOR
Jeremy Mitchell

LEAD DESIGNER
Kelsea Allen

DESIGNERS
Abbey Benson
Davis DeLisi
Annie Glover

MARKETING

MARKETING DIRECTOR
Krista Juline Williams

MARKETING MANAGER
Katie Matuska Pierce

SOCIAL MEDIA MANAGER
Ansley Rushing

COMMUNITY SUPPORT SPECIALIST
Margot Williams

SHIPPING & LOGISTICS

LOGISTICS MANAGER
Lauren Gloyne

SHIPPING MANAGER
Sydney Bess

CUSTOMER SUPPORT SPECIALIST
Katy McKnight

FULFILLMENT SPECIALISTS
Abigail Achord
Cait Baggerman
Kamiren Passavanti

SUBSCRIPTION INQUIRIES
orders@shereadstruth.com

CONTRIBUTORS

PHOTOGRAPHY
Loreal Byers (134)

@SHEREADSTRUTH

Download the She Reads Truth app, available for iOS and Android

Subscribe to the She Reads Truth podcast

SHEREADSTRUTH.COM

SHE READS TRUTH™

© 2020 by She Reads Truth, LLC

All rights reserved.

All photography used by permission.

ISBN 978-1-952670-06-0

1 2 3 4 5 6 7 8 9 10

No part of this publication may be reproduced, distributed, or transmitted in any form or by any means, including photocopying, recording, or other electronic or mechanical methods, without the prior written permission of She Reads Truth, LLC, except in the case of brief quotations embodied in critical reviews and certain other noncommercial uses permitted by copyright law.

Unless otherwise noted, all Scripture is taken from the Christian Standard Bible®. Copyright © 2020 by Holman Bible Publishers. Used by permission. Christian Standard Bible® and CSB® are federally registered trademarks of Holman Bible Publishers.

Scripture quotations marked NASB are taken from the New American Standard Bible® (NASB), Copyright © 1960, 1962, 1963, 1968, 1971, 1972, 1973, 1975, 1977, 1995 by The Lockman Foundation. Used by permission.

Scripture quotations marked NIV are taken from the Holy Bible, New International Version®, NIV®. Copyright © 1973, 1978, 1984, 2011 by Biblica, Inc.™ Used by permission of Zondervan. All rights reserved worldwide. www.zondervan.com. The "NIV" and "New International Version" are trademarks registered in the United States Patent and Trademark Office by Biblica, Inc.™

Research support provided by Logos Bible Software™. Learn more at logos.com.

This book was printed offset in Nashville, Tennessee, on 70# Lynx Opaque. Cover is 100# Cougar Opaque with a soft touch lamination.

FAITH IN PRACTICE

A BIBLICAL STUDY OF SPIRITUAL DISCIPLINES

SHE READS TRUTH

Our highest calling is to walk with the
Lord and live our lives unto Him.

EDITOR'S LETTER

Raechel

Raechel Myers
FOUNDER & CHIEF
EXECUTIVE OFFICER

With hands wrapped around warm mugs at the coffee shop in our little town, Amanda and I sat across the table from our friend and mentor, doing the thing we seemed to do a lot of in the early days of She Reads Truth: asking our pastors for guidance. "We don't know what God is doing with She Reads Truth, but whatever it is, we want to do it well."

We often repeat the advice Dr. Grant gave us that day to one another: "The greatest threat you pose to this community and the world around you is not in the words you write, but in whether or not you live consecrated lives."

Consecrated lives—that is our call as followers of Jesus. Whether we are stewarding a friendship or a family, a platform or a classroom, our highest calling is to walk with the Lord and live our lives unto Him. But what does that look like in practice? We didn't fully understand then, and we don't fully understand now, but we are learning that Paul's instruction to "train yourself in godliness" is not a mysterious calling (1 Timothy 4:7). In Scripture, we find disciplines our living Lord instructed and demonstrated that we can follow in becoming more like Him.

The twenty spiritual disciplines in this book are not exhaustive, and they are not intended to be tackled or mastered all at once. They do not earn us salvation or make God love us more. While we're tempted to aim for "a better prayer life" or even "a consistent Bible reading habit," these important practices are just that—practices. They are not an end unto themselves, but rather a means of knowing God and orienting our lives toward Him.

Friends, I'm not exaggerating when I say this is one of my favorite Study Books our team has ever offered. We want to walk through this study well together, so we've included more extras than usual, like the spiritual inventory on page 20 and the daily and weekly reflection questions you'll encounter as you go. And because putting our faith in practice is so directly tied to being part of a local community of believers, you'll find a look into what Scripture teaches about the Church on page 36.

As women who desire to live lives consecrated to Christ, to train ourselves in godliness, let's approach the coming four weeks eager to learn, ready for our toes to be stepped on a little (or a lot), and most of all, trusting a Person, not a process. Jesus has already given us all we need, including this community of women in the Word of God every day (2 Peter 1:3). Let's be encouraged and encourage one another as we learn together what it looks like to put our faith into practice!

DESIGN ON PURPOSE

At She Reads Truth, we believe in pairing the inherently beautiful Word of God with the aesthetic beauty it deserves. Each of our resources is thoughtfully and artfully designed to highlight the beauty, goodness, and truth of Scripture in a way that reflects the themes of each curated reading plan.

In this Study Book, you'll find soft cream and pink tones punctuated by an active green—the color of Ordinary Time in the Church calendar. This green symbolizes the life-giving rhythms spiritual practices can cultivate in every season.

We took inspiration from planners and bullet journaling in the type and layout design. The dot grids and interactive reflection spreads nod to how these tools bring structure and accountability to new habits in daily life.

Our team paired these structured elements with a freeform lettering style, featured on the Weekly Truth verses and the cover. This organic, unrefined style acts as a reminder that these disciplines are not habits we are meant to perfect; they are part of our always in-process pursuit of following Jesus.

SHE READS TRUTH

We are a community of women dedicated to reading the Word of God every day. The Bible is living and active, and we confidently hold it higher than anything we can do or say.

READ & REFLECT

Spiritual disciplines are not a to-do list or steps in a program. As you work through this Study Book, resist the urge to think of each discipline as a quick fix. Instead, read through each day considering how each practice is an opportunity to live as a disciple of Jesus.

SCRIPTURE READING

Designed for a Monday start, this Study Book presents daily readings on different spiritual disciplines.

At the start of each weekday, you'll find a wayfinding tool that marks each discipline as one of abstinence or engagement. These categories are not rigid, but serve as a framework for understanding how these practices can be incorporated into your life.

Disciplines of **abstinence** are practices of refraining from something.

Disciplines of **engagement** are practices of adding intentional habits into your life.

DAILY REFLECTION

Each weekday concludes with questions about the daily reading and an opportunity to reflect on what that discipline could look like in practice.

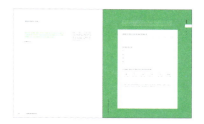

WEEKLY REFLECTION

Each week includes space to plan for incorporating a practice into your weekly rhythm.

COMMUNITY & CONVERSATION

Get the most out of **Faith in Practice** by joining women from Okay, OK, to Oman as they read Truth with you.

GRACE DAY

Use Saturdays to catch up on your reading, pray, and rest in the presence of the Lord.

 ### SHE READS TRUTH APP

Devotionals corresponding to each daily reading in **Faith in Practice** can be found on the She Reads Truth app. You can also participate in community discussions, download free lock screens to help with Weekly Truth memorization, and more!

WEEKLY TRUTH

Sundays are set aside for Scripture memorization.

 ### SHEREADSTRUTH.COM

All of our reading plans and devotionals are available at SheReadsTruth.com. Invite your family, friends, and neighbors to read along with you.

EXTRAS

This book features additional tools to help you gain a deeper understanding of the text.

 ### SHE READS TRUTH PODCAST

Each week, we'll talk about the beauty, goodness, and truth we're finding as we read God's Word together. Subscribe to the podcast and walk away from every episode encouraged to keep opening your Bible.

TABLE OF CONTENTS

1

DAY 1	Living the New Life	22
DAY 2	Study	26
DAY 3	Fellowship	32
DAY 4	Prayer	38
DAY 5	Obedience	44
Weekly Reflection		**48**
DAY 6	Grace Day	50
DAY 7	Weekly Truth	52

2

DAY 8	Service	54
DAY 9	Meditation & Memorization	58
DAY 10	Fasting	62
DAY 11	Sabbath	68
DAY 12	Lament	72
Weekly Reflection		**78**
DAY 13	Grace Day	80
DAY 14	Weekly Truth	82

EXTRAS

What Are Spiritual Disciplines?	16
Spiritual Inventory	20
What Is the Church?	36
Principles for Prayer	42
Active Faith	66
Hymn: Holy, Holy, Holy	92
Faith and Works	126
Benediction	146
Recommended Reading	149
For the Record	152

DAY 15	Celebration	84	DAY 22	Solitude	114
DAY 16	Worship	88	DAY 23	Silence	118
DAY 17	Confession	94	DAY 24	Simplicity	122
DAY 18	Submission	98	DAY 25	Chastity	130
DAY 19	Giving	102	DAY 26	Remembrance	134
Weekly Reflection		**108**	**Weekly Reflection**		**140**
DAY 20	Grace Day	110	DAY 27	Grace Day	142
DAY 21	Weekly Truth	112	DAY 28	Weekly Truth	144

DALLAS WILLARD

The secret of the easy yoke, then, is to learn from Christ how to live our total lives, how to invest all our time and our energies of mind and body as he did.

Train yourself in godliness. For the training of the body has limited benefit, but godliness is beneficial in every way, since it holds promise for the present life and also for the life to come.

KEY VERSE	*1 Timothy 4:7b–8*

WHAT ARE SPIRITUAL DISCIPLINES?

SPIRITUAL DISCIPLINES ARE PRACTICES THAT DEEPEN OUR RELATIONSHIP WITH GOD.

Scripture does not provide us with a succinct list of spiritual disciplines as it does with spiritual gifts or the fruit of the Spirit. However, when we observe the historic habits of God's people, as well as the teaching and example of Jesus and His disciples, we find models for building these habits into the rhythms of our own lives.

SPIRITUAL

"SPIRITUAL" REFERS TO A WAY OF BEING AND LIVING THAT IS CONNECTED TO THE HOLY SPIRIT.

In the book of Galatians, Paul says that if we live by the Spirit, we will "keep in step with the Spirit" (5:25). This communicates a divine partnership, where the Holy Spirit guides our steps and we are called to obey the Spirit's direction as we live out our faith. Similarly, Colossians describes "spiritual understanding" as knowledge of God's will that allows us to walk in a way that is pleasing to the Lord (1:9–10).

DISCIPLINE

"DISCIPLINE" REFERS TO INTENTIONAL, ACTIVE PATTERNS OF BEHAVIOR IN PURSUIT OF GOD'S PRESENCE IN OUR LIVES.

In 1 Timothy, Paul urges us to discipline ourselves "for the purpose of godliness" (4:7 NASB). Like an athlete trains for a marathon through exercise, sleep, and diet, or a musician trains for a recital through practice and preparation over a period of time, we can engage in habits that orient us toward our goal of being more like Christ.

SPIRITUAL DISCIPLINES ARE...

Practices and habits taught or modeled in Scripture.

A means of practicing and seeking God's presence, not an end unto themselves.

Activities experienced both personally and collectively in Christian community.

Beneficial for new and mature believers alike.

SPIRITUAL DISCIPLINES ARE NOT...

Something to accomplish or check off a list.
A type of "advanced" Christianity.
A means of earning God's love or dictating how God will work.
An exhaustive collection of practices for spiritual formation.
A way to add or take away from the work of Jesus.
A guarantee that your life will bear a particular result.

SPIRITUAL INVENTORY

> HOW WE SPEND OUR DAYS IS, OF COURSE, HOW WE SPEND OUR LIVES. WHAT WE DO WITH THIS HOUR, AND THAT ONE, IS WHAT WE ARE DOING.
>
> ANNIE DILLARD

What habits, practices, and influences are already shaping who you are today and who you are becoming? The way we spend our days is the way we spend our lives. And the way we spend our lives reflects what we value most.

Without judgment or condemnation, ask God to make you aware of your life as it is today as you plan to pursue His presence in the coming days and weeks. Use the following prompts to look around and observe what your life says about what you value.

I REGULARLY MAKE TIME TO...

Use different symbols or colors to create a key. Fill in the squares below to reflect on how you spend the hours you've been given each week.

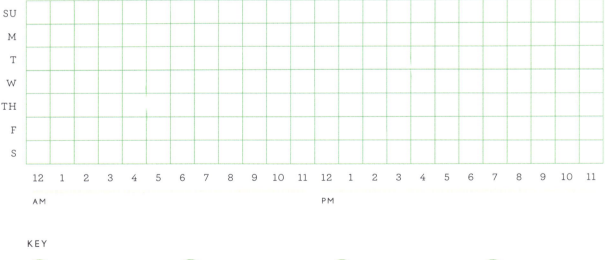

KEY

○ CARE FOR MY BODY

○ SPEND TIME WITH FAMILY AND FRIENDS

○ ATTEND WORK/ SCHOOL

○ CONSUME MEDIA

○ _____

○ _____

○ _____

○ _____

FAITH IN PRACTICE

IN AN AVERAGE WEEK, date   /   /

| I LISTEN TO | I READ | I WATCH |

MY MOST USED APPS ARE

01 _____ 02 _____ 03 _____

I feel most overwhelmed, anxious, or out of control when

I experience joy, peace, patience, and rest when

My relationship with the local church is

I'M MOST AWARE OF GOD WHEN _____

I experience this ○ DAILY ○ WEEKLY ○ MONTHLY ○ ANNUALLY ○ RARELY

MY HOPE FOR THIS STUDY IS

LIVING THE NEW LIFE

DAY 1

"Take up my yoke and learn from me, because I am lowly and humble in heart, and you will find rest for your souls." MATTHEW 11:29

date   /   /

Matthew 11:28–30

28 "Come to me, all of you who are weary and burdened, and I will give you rest. 29 Take up my yoke and learn from me, because I am lowly and humble in heart, and you will find rest for your souls. 30 For my yoke is easy and my burden is light."

Luke 9:23

Then he said to them all, "If anyone wants to follow after me, let him deny himself, take up his cross daily, and follow me."

John 15:1–11
THE VINE AND THE BRANCHES

1 "I am the true vine, and my Father is the gardener. 2 Every branch in me that does not produce fruit he removes, and he prunes every branch that produces fruit so that it will produce more fruit. 3 You are already clean because of the word I have spoken to you. 4 Remain in me, and I in you. Just as a branch is unable to produce fruit by itself unless it remains on the vine, neither can you unless you remain in me. 5 I am the vine; you are the branches. The one who remains in me and I in him produces much fruit, because you can do nothing without me. 6 If anyone does not remain in me, he is thrown aside like a branch and he withers. They gather them, throw them into the fire, and they are burned. 7 If you remain in me and my words remain in you, ask whatever you want and it will be done for you. 8 My Father is glorified by this: that you produce much fruit and prove to be my disciples.

CHRISTLIKE LOVE

9 "As the Father has loved me, I have also loved you. Remain in my love. 10 If you keep my commands you will remain in my love, just as I have kept my Father's commands and remain in his love.

11 "I have told you these things so that my joy may be in you and your joy may be complete."

Ephesians 4:17–24
LIVING THE NEW LIFE

17 Therefore, I say this and testify in the Lord: You should no longer walk as the Gentiles do, in the futility of their thoughts. 18 They are darkened in their understanding, excluded from the life of God, because of the ignorance that is in them and because of the hardness of their hearts. 19 They became callous and gave themselves over to promiscuity for the practice of every kind of impurity with a desire for more and more.

20 But that is not how you came to know Christ, 21 assuming you heard about him and were taught by him, as the truth is in Jesus, 22 to take off your former way of life, the old self that is corrupted by deceitful desires, 23 to be renewed in the spirit of your minds, 24 and to put on the new self, the one created according to God's likeness in righteousness and purity of the truth.

NOTES

Colossians 1:9–14
PRAYER FOR SPIRITUAL GROWTH

⁹ For this reason also, since the day we heard this, we haven't stopped praying for you. We are asking that you may be filled with the knowledge of his will in all wisdom and spiritual understanding, ¹⁰ so that you may walk worthy of the Lord, fully pleasing to him: bearing fruit in every good work and growing in the knowledge of God, ¹¹ being strengthened with all power, according to his glorious might, so that you may have great endurance and patience, joyfully ¹² giving thanks to the Father, who has enabled you to share in the saints' inheritance in the light. ¹³ He has rescued us from the domain of darkness and transferred us into the kingdom of the Son he loves. ¹⁴ In him we have redemption, the forgiveness of sins.

1 Timothy 4:4–16

⁴ For everything created by God is good, and nothing is to be rejected if it is received with thanksgiving, ⁵ since it is sanctified by the word of God and by prayer.

A GOOD SERVANT OF JESUS CHRIST

⁶ If you point these things out to the brothers and sisters, you will be a good servant of Christ Jesus, nourished by the words of the faith and the good teaching that you have followed. ⁷ But have nothing to do with pointless and silly myths. Rather, train yourself in godliness. ⁸ For the training of the body has limited benefit, but godliness is beneficial in every way, since it holds promise for the present life and also for the life to come. ⁹ This saying is trustworthy and deserves full acceptance. ¹⁰ For this reason we labor and strive, because we have put our hope in the living God, who is the Savior of all people, especially of those who believe.

INSTRUCTIONS FOR MINISTRY

¹¹ Command and teach these things. ¹² Don't let anyone despise your youth, but set an example for the believers in speech, in conduct, in love, in faith, and in purity. ¹³ Until I come, give your attention to public reading, exhortation, and teaching. ¹⁴ Don't neglect the gift that is in you; it was given to you through prophecy, with the laying on of hands by the council of elders.

¹⁵ **Practice these things; be committed to them, so that your progress may be evident to all.**

¹⁶ Pay close attention to your life and your teaching; persevere in these things, for in doing this you will save both yourself and your hearers.

DAY 1: LIVING THE NEW LIFE

QUESTIONS FOR REFLECTION

01

Turn to the table of contents on pages 10–11 and look over the different disciplines we will read about in the next four weeks. What is your initial response to the idea of spiritual practices like these?

02

How is life as a follower of Jesus described in today's Scripture reading? How is the local body of believers integral to that life?

We must always remember that the path does not produce the change; it only places us where change can occur.

RICHARD FOSTER

03

When you read about following Jesus, how do you feel?

04

As a person who has put her faith in Jesus, what does it look like to live knowing you have already been accepted and redeemed by Jesus? How is this different than following rules in pursuit of approval?

DAY 2

STUDY

The practice of exploring and deepening your understanding of God's Word.

date   /   /

Ezra 7:8–10

⁸ Ezra came to Jerusalem in the fifth month, during the seventh year of the king. ⁹ He began the journey from Babylon on the first day of the first month and arrived in Jerusalem on the first day of the fifth month since the gracious hand of his God was on him. ¹⁰ Now Ezra had determined in his heart to study the law of the LORD, obey it, and teach its statutes and ordinances in Israel.

Nehemiah 8

¹ All the people gathered together at the square in front of the Water Gate. They asked the scribe Ezra to bring the book of the law of Moses that the LORD had given Israel. ² On the first day of the seventh month, the priest Ezra brought the law before the assembly of men, women, and all who could listen with understanding. ³ While he was facing the square in front of the Water Gate, he read out of it from daybreak until noon before the men, the women, and those who could understand. All the people listened attentively to the book of the law. ⁴ The scribe Ezra stood on a high wooden platform made for this purpose. Mattithiah, Shema, Anaiah, Uriah, Hilkiah, and Maaseiah stood beside him on his right; to his left were Pedaiah, Mishael, Malchijah, Hashum, Hashbaddanah, Zechariah, and Meshullam. ⁵ Ezra opened the book in full view of all the people, since he was elevated above everyone. As he opened it, all the people stood up. ⁶ Ezra blessed the LORD, the great God, and with their hands uplifted all the people said, "Amen, Amen!" Then they knelt low and worshiped the LORD with their faces to the ground.

⁷ Jeshua, Bani, Sherebiah, Jamin, Akkub, Shabbethai, Hodiah, Maaseiah, Kelita, Azariah, Jozabad, Hanan, and Pelaiah, who were Levites, explained the law to the people as they stood in their places. ⁸ They read out of the book of the law of God, translating and giving the meaning so that the people could understand what was read. ⁹ Nehemiah the governor, Ezra the priest and scribe, and the Levites who were instructing the people said to all of them, "This day is holy to the LORD your God. Do not mourn or weep." For all the people were weeping as they heard the words of the law. ¹⁰ Then he said to them, "Go and eat what is rich, drink what is sweet, and send portions to those who have nothing prepared, since today is holy to our Lord. Do not grieve, because the joy of the LORD is your strength." ¹¹ And the Levites quieted all the people, saying, "Be still, since today is holy. Don't grieve." ¹² Then all the people began to eat and drink, send portions, and have a great celebration, because they had understood the words that were explained to them.

FESTIVAL OF SHELTERS OBSERVED

¹³ On the second day, the family heads of all the people, along with the priests and Levites, assembled before the scribe Ezra to study the words of the law. ¹⁴ They found written in the law how the LORD had commanded through Moses that the Israelites should dwell in shelters during the festival of the seventh month. ¹⁵ So they proclaimed and spread this news throughout their towns and in Jerusalem, saying, "Go out to the hill country and bring back branches of olive, wild olive, myrtle, palm, and other leafy trees to make shelters, just as it is written." ¹⁶ The people went out, brought back branches, and made shelters for themselves on each of their rooftops and courtyards, the court of the house of God, the square by the Water Gate, and the square by the Ephraim Gate. ¹⁷ The whole community that had returned from exile made shelters and lived in them. The Israelites had not celebrated like this from the days of Joshua son of Nun until that day. And there was tremendous joy. ¹⁸ Ezra read out of the book of the law of God every day, from the first day to the last. The Israelites celebrated the festival for seven days, and on the eighth day there was a solemn assembly, according to the ordinance.

Psalm 111:1–4
PRAISE FOR THE LORD'S WORKS

¹ Hallelujah!
I will praise the LORD with all my heart
in the assembly of the upright and in the congregation.
² The LORD's works are great,
studied by all who delight in them.
³ All that he does is splendid and majestic;
his righteousness endures forever.
⁴ He has caused his wondrous works to be remembered.
The LORD is gracious and compassionate.

Luke 2:41–52
IN HIS FATHER'S HOUSE

⁴¹ Every year his parents traveled to Jerusalem for the Passover Festival. ⁴² When he was twelve years old, they went up according to the custom of the festival. ⁴³ After those days were over, as they were returning, the boy Jesus stayed behind in Jerusalem, but his parents did not know it. ⁴⁴ Assuming he was in the traveling party, they went a day's journey. Then they began looking for him among their relatives and friends. ⁴⁵ When they did not find him, they returned to Jerusalem to search for him. ⁴⁶ After three days, they found him in the temple sitting among the teachers, listening to them and asking them questions. ⁴⁷ And all those who heard him were astounded at his understanding and his answers. ⁴⁸ When his parents saw him, they were astonished, and his mother said to him, "Son, why have you treated us like this? Your father and I have been anxiously searching for you."

⁴⁹ "Why were you searching for me?" he asked them. "Didn't you know that it was necessary for me to be in my Father's house?" ⁵⁰ But they did not understand what he said to them.

IN FAVOR WITH GOD AND WITH PEOPLE

⁵¹ Then he went down with them and came to Nazareth and was obedient to them. His mother kept all these things in her heart. ⁵² And Jesus increased in wisdom and stature, and in favor with God and with people.

2 Timothy 2:14–19

¹⁴ Remind them of these things, and charge them before God not to fight about words. This is useless and leads to the ruin of those who listen.

¹⁵ Be diligent to present yourself to God as one approved, a worker who doesn't need to be ashamed, correctly teaching the word of truth.

¹⁶ Avoid irreverent and empty speech, since those who engage in it will produce even more godlessness, ¹⁷ and their teaching will spread like gangrene. Hymenaeus and Philetus are among them. ¹⁸ They have departed from the

truth, saying that the resurrection has already taken place, and are ruining the faith of some. ⁱ⁹ Nevertheless, God's solid foundation stands firm, bearing this inscription: The Lord knows those who are his, and let everyone who calls on the name of the Lord turn away from wickedness.

Hebrews 4:12
For the word of God is living and effective and sharper than any double-edged sword, penetrating as far as the separation of soul and spirit, joints and marrow. It is able to judge the thoughts and intentions of the heart.

NOTES

DAY 2: STUDY

QUESTIONS FOR REFLECTION

01

How is the discipline of study taught by Jesus? How is it discussed in Scripture?

02

How does today's Scripture reading change your understanding of study? How have you seen study modeled in a healthy way? How have you seen it misused or distorted?

The ultimate benefit of firsthand Bible study is that you will fall in love with the Author. You see, it's hard to fall in love by proxy...If you want to know God directly, you need to encounter His Word directly.

HOWARD HENDRICKS

03

What fruit could come from practicing this discipline?

04

What could it look like to incorporate the practice of study into your life?

DAY 3

FELLOWSHIP

The practice of living in community and engaging in spiritual disciplines corporately with other believers.

date   /   /

Luke 7:34–48

34 "The Son of Man has come eating and drinking, and you say, 'Look, a glutton and a drunkard, a friend of tax collectors and sinners!' 35 Yet wisdom is vindicated by all her children."

MUCH FORGIVENESS, MUCH LOVE

36 Then one of the Pharisees invited him to eat with him. He entered the Pharisee's house and reclined at the table. 37 And a woman in the town who was a sinner found out that Jesus was reclining at the table in the Pharisee's house. She brought an alabaster jar of perfume 38 and stood behind him at his feet, weeping, and began to wash his feet with her tears. She wiped his feet with her hair, kissing them and anointing them with the perfume.

39 When the Pharisee who had invited him saw this, he said to himself, "This man, if he were a prophet, would know who and what kind of woman this is who is touching him—she's a sinner!"

40 Jesus replied to him, "Simon, I have something to say to you."

He said, "Say it, teacher."

41 "A creditor had two debtors. One owed five hundred denarii, and the other fifty. 42 Since they could not pay it back, he graciously forgave them both. So, which of them will love him more?"

43 Simon answered, "I suppose the one he forgave more."

"You have judged correctly," he told him. 44 Turning to the woman, he said to Simon, "Do you see this woman? I entered your house; you gave me no water for my feet, but she, with her tears, has washed my feet and wiped them with her hair. 45 You gave me no kiss, but she hasn't stopped kissing my feet since I came in. 46 You didn't anoint my head with olive oil, but she has anointed my feet with perfume. 47 Therefore I tell you, her many sins have been forgiven; that's why she loved much. But the one who is forgiven little, loves little." 48 Then he said to her, "Your sins are forgiven."

Acts 2:42–47
A GENEROUS AND GROWING CHURCH

42 They devoted themselves to the apostles' teaching, to the fellowship, to the breaking of bread, and to prayer.

43 Everyone was filled with awe, and many wonders and signs were being performed through the apostles. 44 Now all the believers were together and held all things in common. 45 They sold their possessions and property and distributed the proceeds to all, as any had need. 46 Every day they devoted themselves to meeting together in the temple, and broke bread from house to house. They ate their food with joyful and sincere hearts, 47 praising God and enjoying the favor of all the people. Every day the Lord added to their number those who were being saved.

Romans 14:13–23
THE LAW OF LOVE

13 Therefore, let us no longer judge one another. Instead decide never to put a stumbling block or pitfall in the way of your brother or sister. 14 I know and am persuaded in the Lord Jesus that nothing is unclean in itself. Still, to someone

who considers a thing to be unclean, to that one it is unclean. ¹⁵ For if your brother or sister is hurt by what you eat, you are no longer walking according to love. Do not destroy, by what you eat, someone for whom Christ died. ¹⁶ Therefore, do not let your good be slandered, ¹⁷ for the kingdom of God is not eating and drinking, but righteousness, peace, and joy in the Holy Spirit. ¹⁸ Whoever serves Christ in this way is acceptable to God and receives human approval.

¹⁹ So then, let us pursue what promotes peace and what builds up one another.

²⁰ Do not tear down God's work because of food. Everything is clean, but it is wrong to make someone fall by what he eats. ²¹ It is a good thing not to eat meat, or drink wine, or do anything that makes your brother or sister stumble. ²² Whatever you believe about these things, keep between yourself and God. Blessed is the one who does not condemn himself by what he approves. ²³ But whoever doubts stands condemned if he eats, because his eating is not from faith, and everything that is not from faith is sin.

1 Corinthians 12:12–26
UNITY YET DIVERSITY IN THE BODY

¹² For just as the body is one and has many parts, and all the parts of that body, though many, are one body—so also is Christ. ¹³ For we were all baptized by one Spirit into one body—whether Jews or Greeks, whether slaves or free—and we were all given one Spirit to drink. ¹⁴ Indeed, the body is not one part but many. ¹⁵ If the foot should say, "Because I'm not a hand, I don't belong to the body," it is not for that reason any less a part of the body. ¹⁶ And if the ear should say, "Because I'm not an eye, I don't belong to the body," it is not for that reason any less a part of the body. ¹⁷ If the whole body were an eye, where would the hearing be? If the whole body were an ear, where would the sense of smell be? ¹⁸ But as it is, God has arranged each one of the parts in the body just as he wanted. ¹⁹ And if they were all the same part, where would the body be? ²⁰ As it is, there are many parts, but one body. ²¹ The eye cannot say to the hand, "I don't need you!" Or again, the head can't say to the feet, "I don't need you!" ²² On the contrary, those parts of the body that are weaker are indispensable. ²³ And those parts of the body that we consider less honorable, we clothe these with greater honor, and our unrespectable parts are treated with greater respect, ²⁴ which our respectable parts do not need.

Instead, God has put the body together, giving greater honor to the less honorable, ²⁵ so that there would be no division in the body, but that the members would have the same concern for each other. ²⁶ So if one member suffers, all the members suffer with it; if one member is honored, all the members rejoice with it.

2 Corinthians 6:14–18
SEPARATION TO GOD

¹⁴ Do not be yoked together with those who do not believe. For what partnership is there between righteousness and lawlessness? Or what fellowship does light have with darkness? ¹⁵ What agreement does Christ have with Belial? Or what does a believer have in common with an unbeliever? ¹⁶ And what agreement does the temple of God have with idols? For we are the temple of the living God, as God said:

> I will dwell
> and walk among them,
> and I will be their God,
> and they will be my people.
> ¹⁷ Therefore, come out from among them
> and be separate, says the Lord;
> do not touch any unclean thing,
> and I will welcome you.
> ¹⁸ And I will be a Father to you,
> and you will be sons and daughters to me,
> says the Lord Almighty.

Hebrews 10:24–25

²⁴ And let us consider one another in order to provoke love and good works, ²⁵ not neglecting to gather together, as some are in the habit of doing, but encouraging each other, and all the more as you see the day approaching.

DAY 3: FELLOWSHIP

QUESTIONS FOR REFLECTION

01

How is the discipline of fellowship taught by Jesus? How is it discussed in Scripture?

02

How does today's Scripture reading change your understanding of fellowship? How have you seen fellowship modeled in a healthy way? How have you seen it misused or distorted?

No one person can fulfill all your needs. But the community can truly hold you. The community can let you experience the fact that, beyond your anguish, there are human hands that hold you and show you God's faithful love.

— HENRI NOUWEN

03

What fruit could come from practicing this discipline?

04

What could it look like to incorporate the practice of fellowship into your life?

WHAT IS THE CHURCH?

Life as the people of God is not meant to be a solitary journey. Rather, Scripture instructs that we, as believers, follow after Jesus together. Likewise, the practice of spiritual disciplines is not meant for private spirituality, but to invite us into a deeper relationship with God and with the body of Christ.

Different metaphors for the community of believers are used throughout the New Testament to help us understand the definition and function of the Church.

THE FAMILY OF GOD

"Whoever does the will of my Father in heaven is my brother and sister and mother." MT 12:50

We are God's children, and if children, also heirs—heirs of God and coheirs with Christ. RM 8:16-17

"And I will be a Father to you, and you will be sons and daughters to me." 2CO 6:18

Let us work for the good of all, especially for those who belong to the household of faith. GL 6:10

See what great love the Father has given us that we should be called God's children—and we are! 1JN 3:1

THE BODY OF CHRIST

As it is, there are many parts, but one body. 1CO 12:20

Now you are the body of Christ, and individual members of it. 1CO 12:27

…to equip the saints for the work of ministry, to build up the body of Christ… EPH 4:12

He is also the head of the body, the church. COL 1:18

THE BRIDE OF CHRIST

I have promised you in marriage to one husband—to present a pure virgin to Christ. 2CO 11:2

…just as Christ loved the church and gave himself for her to make her holy. EPH 5:25-26

The marriage of the Lamb has come, and his bride has prepared herself. RV 19:7

THE LIGHT OF THE WORLD

"You are the light of the world. A city situated on a hill cannot be hidden." MT 5:14

The seven lampstands are the seven churches. RV 1:20

THE PEOPLE OF GOD

Our citizenship is in heaven. PHP 3:20

But you are a chosen race, a royal priesthood, a holy nation, a people for his possession… 1PT 2:9

To him who loves us…and made us a kingdom, priests to his God and Father—to him be the glory and dominion forever and ever. RV 1:5-6

They will be his peoples, and God himself will be with them and will be their God. RV 21:3

THE HOUSE OF GOD

You are no longer foreigners and strangers, but fellow citizens with the saints, and members of God's household. EPH 2:19

…God's household, which is the church… 1TM 3:15

Christ was faithful as a Son over his household. And we are that household… HEB 3:6

…you yourselves, as living stones, a spiritual house, are being built to be a holy priesthood… 1PT 2:5

THE TEMPLE OF THE SPIRIT

…you are God's temple and that the Spirit of God lives in you… 1CO 3:16

For we are the temple of the living God. 2CO 6:16

In him you are also being built together for God's dwelling in the Spirit. EPH 2:22

THE FLOCK

"Don't be afraid, little flock, because your Father delights to give you the kingdom." LK 12:32

"I am the good shepherd. The good shepherd lays down his life for the sheep." JN 10:11

Be on guard for yourselves and for all the flock of which the Holy Spirit has appointed you as overseers, to shepherd the church of God. AC 20:28

…our Lord Jesus—the great Shepherd of the sheep… HEB 13:20

CHRIST'S LETTER

You show that you are Christ's letter, delivered by us, not written with ink but with the Spirit of the living God—not on tablets of stone but on tablets of human hearts. 2CO 3:3

DAY 4

PRAYER

DISCIPLINE OF ENGAGEMENT

The practice of talking with God through rhythms of speaking and listening.

date   /   /

Matthew 6:5–13
HOW TO PRAY

⁵ "Whenever you pray, you must not be like the hypocrites, because they love to pray standing in the synagogues and on the street corners to be seen by people. Truly I tell you, they have their reward. ⁶ But when you pray, go into your private room, shut your door, and pray to your Father who is in secret. And your Father who sees in secret will reward you. ⁷ When you pray, don't babble like the Gentiles, since they imagine they'll be heard for their many words. ⁸ Don't be like them, because your Father knows the things you need before you ask him.

THE LORD'S PRAYER

⁹ "Therefore, you should pray like this:

Our Father in heaven,
your name be honored as holy.
¹⁰ Your kingdom come.
Your will be done
on earth as it is in heaven.
¹¹ Give us today our daily bread.
¹² And forgive us our debts,
as we also have forgiven our debtors.
¹³ And do not bring us into temptation,
but deliver us from the evil one."

Luke 18:1–14

¹ Now he told them a parable on the need for them to pray always and not give up. ² "There was a judge in a certain town who didn't fear God or respect people. ³ And a widow in that town kept coming to him, saying, 'Give me justice against my adversary.'

⁴ "For a while he was unwilling, but later he said to himself, 'Even though I don't fear God or respect people, ⁵ yet because this widow keeps pestering me, I will give her justice, so that she doesn't wear me out by her persistent coming.'"

⁶ Then the Lord said, "Listen to what the unjust judge says. ⁷ Will not God grant justice to his elect who cry out to him day and night? Will he delay helping them? ⁸ I tell you that he will swiftly grant them justice. Nevertheless, when the Son of Man comes, will he find faith on earth?"

THE PARABLE OF THE PHARISEE AND THE TAX COLLECTOR

⁹ He also told this parable to some who trusted in themselves that they were righteous and looked down on everyone else: ¹⁰ "Two men went up to the temple to pray, one a Pharisee and the other a tax collector. ¹¹ The Pharisee was standing and praying like this about himself: 'God, I thank you that I'm not like other people—greedy, unrighteous, adulterers, or even like this tax collector. ¹² I fast twice a week; I give a tenth of everything I get.'

¹³ "But the tax collector, standing far off, would not even raise his eyes to heaven but kept striking his chest and saying, 'God, have mercy on me, a sinner!' ¹⁴ I tell you, this one went down to his house justified rather than the other, because everyone who exalts himself will be humbled, but the one who humbles himself will be exalted."

John 15:7

"If you remain in me and my words remain in you, ask whatever you want and it will be done for you."

Romans 12:12

Rejoice in hope; be patient in affliction; be persistent in prayer.

Hebrews 4:14–16
OUR GREAT HIGH PRIEST

¹⁴ Therefore, since we have a great high priest who has passed through the heavens—Jesus the Son of God—let us hold fast to our confession. ¹⁵ For we do not have a high priest who is unable to sympathize with our weaknesses, but one who has been tempted in every way as we are, yet without sin. ¹⁶ Therefore, let us approach the throne of grace with boldness, so that we may receive mercy and find grace to help us in time of need.

DAY 4: PRAYER

QUESTIONS FOR REFLECTION

01

How is the discipline of prayer taught by Jesus? How is it discussed in Scripture?

02

How does today's Scripture reading change your understanding of prayer? How have you seen prayer modeled in a healthy way? How have you seen it misused or distorted?

*If you are searching for God and do not know where to begin,
learn to pray and take the trouble to pray every day.*

MOTHER TERESA

03

What fruit could come from practicing this discipline?

04

What could it look like to incorporate the practice of prayer into your life?

PRINCIPLES FOR PRAYER

How should we pray? What should we keep in mind as we do? Practicing the art of prayer is one of the great rewards of following Jesus over the course of a lifetime. Prayer is a conversation with God and should be part of every discipline we engage.

REMEMBER

With God, all things are possible.
MK 10:27

Jesus is our Great High Priest who is always interceding for us.
HEB 7:24-25

The Holy Spirit lives in the hearts of all believers.
1CO 3:16

God sees things perfectly, even when we can't. Our personal feelings do not dictate what is actually true.
EPH 1:18

God is gracious and compassionate.
PS 145:8

God has already proven the depth of His love for us by giving us His Son.
JN 3:16

Prayer should be honest; God already knows our hearts.
AC 15:8

Prayer requires faith.
MT 21:22

Prayer is a form of worship.
PS 29:1-2

Prayer is not meant to be a performance.
MT 6:5-6

Prayer is meant to change us.
PS 119:26-27

PRACTICE

Being quiet in prayer in order to listen as much as you speak.
MT 6:6; RM 8:26

Reading Scripture when you pray. It is God's Word to us.
RM 10:17

Praying in Jesus's name, acknowledging that He is the only way we can approach God.
JN 14:6

Asking for the Holy Spirit's help.
RM 8:26-27

Revering God's name, and using Scripture to expand your vocabulary in terms of how you address Him.
IS 9:6; MT 6:9

Asking God to help you examine your own heart as you pray.
PS 26:2

Confessing sin and accepting forgiveness.
LK 18:13

Planning by setting aside time for prayer and Scripture reading.
MK 1:35

Praying spontaneous, simple prayers throughout the day.
1TH 5:17-18

Asking God for what you need and being willing to ask more than once.
MT 7:9-11; LK 18:4-8

Praying for others, not just yourself.
PHP 2:3-4

Giving thanks to God.
PHP 4:6

DAY 5

OBEDIENCE

The practice of seeking God's will, both individually and in community, and acting in agreement with it.

date   /   /

Isaiah 58:11
The Lord will always lead you,
satisfy you in a parched land,
and strengthen your bones.
You will be like a watered garden
and like a spring whose water never runs dry.

John 10:1–15
THE GOOD SHEPHERD

[1] "Truly I tell you, anyone who doesn't enter the sheep pen by the gate but climbs in some other way is a thief and a robber. [2] The one who enters by the gate is the shepherd of the sheep. [3] The gatekeeper opens it for him, and the sheep hear his voice. He calls his own sheep by name and leads them out. [4] When he has brought all his own outside, he goes ahead of them. The sheep follow him because they know his voice. [5] They will never follow a stranger; instead they will run away from him, because they don't know the voice of strangers." [6] Jesus gave them this figure of speech, but they did not understand what he was telling them.

[7] Jesus said again, "Truly I tell you, I am the gate for the sheep. [8] All who came before me are thieves and robbers, but the sheep didn't listen to them. [9] I am the gate. If anyone enters by me, he will be saved and will come in and go out and find pasture. [10] A thief comes only to steal and kill and destroy. I have come so that they may have life and have it in abundance.

[11] "I am the good shepherd. The good shepherd lays down his life for the sheep. [12] The hired hand, since he is not the shepherd and doesn't own the sheep, leaves them and runs away when he sees a wolf coming. The wolf then snatches and scatters them. [13] This happens because he is a hired hand and doesn't care about the sheep.

[14] "I am the good shepherd. I know my own, and my own know me, [15] just as the Father knows me, and I know the Father. I lay down my life for the sheep."

John 14:15–26
ANOTHER COUNSELOR PROMISED

[15] "If you love me, you will keep my commands. [16] And I will ask the Father, and he will give you another Counselor to be with you forever. [17] He is the Spirit of truth. The world is unable to receive him because it doesn't see him or know him. But you do know him, because he remains with you and will be in you.

THE FATHER, THE SON, AND THE HOLY SPIRIT

[18] "I will not leave you as orphans; I am coming to you. [19] In a little while the world will no longer see me, but you will see me. Because I live, you will live too. [20] On that day you will know that I am in my Father, you are in me, and I am in you. [21] The one who has my commands and keeps them is the one who loves me. And the one who loves me will be loved by my Father. I also will love him and will reveal myself to him."

NOTES

²² Judas (not Iscariot) said to him, "Lord, how is it you're going to reveal yourself to us and not to the world?"

²³ Jesus answered, "If anyone loves me, he will keep my word. My Father will love him, and we will come to him and make our home with him. ²⁴ The one who doesn't love me will not keep my words. The word that you hear is not mine but is from the Father who sent me.

²⁵ "I have spoken these things to you while I remain with you. ²⁶ But the Counselor, the Holy Spirit, whom the Father will send in my name, will teach you all things and remind you of everything I have told you."

Acts 16:6–10

⁶ They went through the region of Phrygia and Galatia; they had been forbidden by the Holy Spirit to speak the word in Asia. ⁷ When they came to Mysia, they tried to go into Bithynia, but the Spirit of Jesus did not allow them. ⁸ Passing by Mysia they went down to Troas. ⁹ During the night Paul had a vision in which a Macedonian man was standing and pleading with him, "Cross over to Macedonia and help us!" ¹⁰ After he had seen the vision, we immediately made efforts to set out for Macedonia, concluding that God had called us to preach the gospel to them.

Galatians 5:25

If we live by the Spirit, let us also keep in step with the Spirit.

James 1:5–6

⁵ Now if any of you lacks wisdom, he should ask God—who gives to all generously and ungrudgingly—and it will be given to him. ⁶ But let him ask in faith without doubting. For the doubter is like the surging sea, driven and tossed by the wind.

DAY 5: OBEDIENCE

QUESTIONS FOR REFLECTION

01

How is the discipline of obedience taught by Jesus? How is it discussed in Scripture?

02

How does today's Scripture reading change your understanding of obedience? How have you seen obedience modeled in a healthy way? How have you seen it misused or distorted?

*For obedience is not stodgy plodding in the ruts of religion,
it is a hopeful race towards God's promises.*

EUGENE PETERSON

03

What fruit could come from practicing this discipline?

04

What could it look like to incorporate the practice of obedience into your life?

| WEEKLY REFLECTION | date / / |

"Remain in me, and I in you. Just as a branch is unable to produce fruit by itself unless it remains on the vine, neither can you unless you remain in me."

JOHN 15:4

Reflect on what you've learned this week. What in the reading grabbed your attention? Which practices felt like an opportunity to cultivate the sort of relationship with God your heart longs for?

Choose a discipline you read about in this first week to intentionally practice in the week ahead. Remember, spiritual disciplines are not a means of salvation or a spiritual to-do list. They are an invitation to embrace God's presence in new ways and deepen or awaken your relationship with Him. Use the space below to plan how you can incorporate this practice into your coming week.

WEEK

1
2
3
4

I WANT TO PRACTICE THE DISCIPLINE OF

I'LL PRACTICE BY

01
02
03
04

I'LL MAKE SPACE TO PRACTICE THIS DISCIPLINE

M	T	W	TH	F	S/SU
am / pm	am / pm	am / pm	am / pm	am / pm	am / pm

Write a short prayer thanking God for your life as His disciple. Ask Him to guide you in your practice as you seek to know and experience Him more.

DAY 6

GRACE DAY

Take this day to catch up on your reading, pray, and rest in the presence of the Lord.

Practice these things; be committed to them, so that your progress may be evident to all.

1 TIMOTHY 4:15

NOTES | date   /   /

DAY 7 | # WEEKLY TRUTH

date / /

Scripture is God-breathed and true. When we memorize it, we carry the good news of Jesus with us wherever we go.

Over the course of this study, we will memorize 1 Timothy 4:7b–9. This week, focus on memorizing verse 7 and the first part of verse 8. You can also download the free lock screen in the She Reads Truth app and read these words out loud whenever you pick up your phone.

> Train yourself in godliness. For the training of the body has limited benefit, but godliness is beneficial in every way, since it holds promise for the present life and also for the life to come. This saying is trustworthy and deserves full acceptance.

—1 TIMOTHY 4:7b–9

DAY 8

SERVICE

The practice of humbling yourself to be present with others and responsive to their needs.

date   /   /

Jeremiah 29:4–7

⁴ This is what the Lord of Armies, the God of Israel, says to all the exiles I deported from Jerusalem to Babylon: ⁵ "Build houses and live in them. Plant gardens and eat their produce. ⁶ Find wives for yourselves, and have sons and daughters. Find wives for your sons and give your daughters to men in marriage so that they may bear sons and daughters. Multiply there; do not decrease. ⁷ Pursue the well-being of the city I have deported you to. Pray to the Lord on its behalf, for when it thrives, you will thrive."

Matthew 20:25–28

²⁵ Jesus called them over and said, "You know that the rulers of the Gentiles lord it over them, and those in high positions act as tyrants over them. ²⁶ It must not be like that among you. On the contrary, whoever wants to become great among you must be your servant, ²⁷ and whoever wants to be first among you must be your slave; ²⁸ just as the Son of Man did not come to be served, but to serve, and to give his life as a ransom for many."

Matthew 22:34–40

³⁴ When the Pharisees heard that he had silenced the Sadducees, they came together. ³⁵ And one of them, an expert in the law, asked a question to test him: ³⁶ "Teacher, which command in the law is the greatest?"

³⁷ He said to him, "Love the Lord your God with all your heart, with all your soul, and with all your mind. ³⁸ This is the greatest and most important command. ³⁹ The second is like it: Love your neighbor as yourself. ⁴⁰ All the Law and the Prophets depend on these two commands."

Matthew 25:31–46
THE SHEEP AND THE GOATS

³¹ "When the Son of Man comes in his glory, and all the angels with him. then he will sit on his glorious throne. ³² All the nations will be gathered before him, and he will separate them one from another, just as a shepherd separates the sheep from the goats. ³³ He will put the sheep on his right and the goats on the left. ³⁴ Then the King will say to those on his right, 'Come, you who are blessed by my Father; inherit the kingdom prepared for you from the foundation of the world.

³⁵ "'For I was hungry and you gave me something to eat; I was thirsty and you gave me something to drink; I was a stranger and you took me in; ³⁶ I was naked and you clothed me; I was sick and you took care of me; I was in prison and you visited me.'

³⁷ "Then the righteous will answer him, 'Lord, when did we see you hungry and feed you, or thirsty and give you

something to drink? ³⁸ When did we see you a stranger and take you in, or without clothes and clothe you? ³⁹ When did we see you sick, or in prison, and visit you?'

⁴⁰ "And the King will answer them, 'Truly I tell you, whatever you did for one of the least of these brothers and sisters of mine, you did for me.'

⁴¹ "Then he will also say to those on the left, 'Depart from me, you who are cursed, into the eternal fire prepared for the devil and his angels! ⁴² For I was hungry and you gave me nothing to eat; I was thirsty and you gave me nothing to drink; ⁴³ I was a stranger and you didn't take me in; I was naked and you didn't clothe me, sick and in prison and you didn't take care of me.'

⁴⁴ "Then they too will answer, 'Lord, when did we see you hungry, or thirsty, or a stranger, or without clothes, or sick, or in prison, and not help you?'

⁴⁵ "Then he will answer them, 'Truly I tell you, whatever you did not do for one of the least of these, you did not do for me.'

⁴⁶ "And they will go away into eternal punishment, but the righteous into eternal life."

John 13:1–17
JESUS WASHES HIS DISCIPLES' FEET

¹ Before the Passover Festival, Jesus knew that his hour had come to depart from this world to the Father.

Having loved his own who were in the world, he loved them to the end.

² Now when it was time for supper, the devil had already put it into the heart of Judas, Simon Iscariot's son, to betray him. ³ Jesus knew that the Father had given everything into his hands, that he had come from God, and that he was going back to God. ⁴ So he got up from supper, laid aside his outer clothing, took a towel, and tied it around himself. ⁵ Next, he poured water into a basin and began to wash his disciples' feet and to dry them with the towel tied around him.

⁶ He came to Simon Peter, who asked him, "Lord, are you going to wash my feet?"

⁷ Jesus answered him, "What I'm doing you don't realize now, but afterward you will understand."

⁸ "You will never wash my feet," Peter said.

Jesus replied, "If I don't wash you, you have no part with me."

⁹ Simon Peter said to him, "Lord, not only my feet, but also my hands and my head."

¹⁰ "One who has bathed," Jesus told him, "doesn't need to wash anything except his feet, but he is completely clean. You are clean, but not all of you." ¹¹ For he knew who would betray him. This is why he said, "Not all of you are clean."

THE MEANING OF FOOT WASHING

¹² When Jesus had washed their feet and put on his outer clothing, he reclined again and said to them, "Do you know what I have done for you? ¹³ You call me Teacher and Lord—and you are speaking rightly, since that is what I am. ¹⁴ So if I, your Lord and Teacher, have washed your feet, you also ought to wash one another's feet. ¹⁵ For I have given you an example, that you also should do just as I have done for you.

¹⁶ "Truly I tell you, a servant is not greater than his master, and a messenger is not greater than the one who sent him. ¹⁷ If you know these things, you are blessed if you do them."

1 John 3:16–18

¹⁶ This is how we have come to know love: He laid down his life for us. We should also lay down our lives for our brothers and sisters. ¹⁷ If anyone has this world's goods and sees a fellow believer in need but withholds compassion from him—how does God's love reside in him? ¹⁸ Little children, let us not love in word or speech, but in action and in truth.

DAY 8: SERVICE

QUESTIONS FOR REFLECTION

01

How is the discipline of service taught by Jesus? How is it discussed in Scripture?

02

How does today's Scripture reading change your understanding of service? How have you seen service modeled in a healthy way? How have you seen it misused or distorted?

> *Everybody can be great, because everybody can serve. You don't have to have a college degree to serve. You don't have to make your subject and your verb agree to serve…You only need a heart full of grace, a soul generated by love.*
>
> **MARTIN LUTHER KING, JR.**

03

What fruit could come from practicing this discipline?

04

What could it look like to incorporate the practice of service into your life?

DAY 9

MEDITATION & MEMORIZATION

The practice of reflecting on Scripture, and the practice of committing it to memory.

date   /   /

Deuteronomy 6:1–9

¹ This is the command—the statutes and ordinances—the Lord your God has commanded me to teach you, so that you may follow them in the land you are about to enter and possess. ² Do this so that you may fear the Lord your God all the days of your life by keeping all his statutes and commands I am giving you, your son, and your grandson, and so that you may have a long life. ³ Listen, Israel, and be careful to follow them, so that you may prosper and multiply greatly, because the Lord, the God of your ancestors, has promised you a land flowing with milk and honey.

⁴ Listen, Israel: The Lord our God, the Lord is one. ⁵ Love the Lord your God with all your heart, with all your soul, and with all your strength. ⁶ These words that I am giving you today are to be in your heart. ⁷ Repeat them to your children. Talk about them when you sit in your house and when you walk along the road, when you lie down and when you get up. ⁸ Bind them as a sign on your hand and let them be a symbol on your forehead. ⁹ Write them on the doorposts of your house and on your city gates.

Psalm 1:1–3
THE TWO WAYS

¹ How happy is the one who does not
walk in the advice of the wicked
or stand in the pathway with sinners
or sit in the company of mockers!

**² Instead, his delight is in the
  Lord's instruction,
and he meditates on it day and night.**

³ He is like a tree planted beside flowing streams
that bears its fruit in its season,
and its leaf does not wither.
Whatever he does prospers.

Psalm 119:11

I have treasured your word in my heart
so that I may not sin against you.

Matthew 4:1–11

¹ Then Jesus was led up by the Spirit into the wilderness to be tempted by the devil. ² After he had fasted forty days and forty nights, he was hungry. ³ Then the tempter approached him and said, "If you are the Son of God, tell these stones to become bread."

⁴ He answered, "It is written: Man must not live on bread alone but on every word that comes from the mouth of God."

⁵ Then the devil took him to the holy city, had him stand on the pinnacle of the temple, ⁶ and said to him, "If you are the Son of God, throw yourself down. For it is written:

He will give his angels orders concerning you,
  and they will support you with their hands
so that you will not strike
  your foot against a stone."

⁷ Jesus told him, "It is also written: Do not test the Lord your God."

⁸ Again, the devil took him to a very high mountain and showed him all the kingdoms of the world and their splendor. ⁹ And he said to him, "I will give you all these things if you will fall down and worship me."

¹⁰ Then Jesus told him, "Go away, Satan! For it is written: Worship the Lord your God, and serve only him."

¹¹ Then the devil left him, and angels came and began to serve him.

2 Timothy 3:14–17

¹⁴ But as for you, continue in what you have learned and firmly believed. You know those who taught you, ¹⁵ and you know that from infancy you have known the sacred Scriptures, which are able to give you wisdom for salvation through faith in Christ Jesus. ¹⁶ All Scripture is inspired by God and is profitable for teaching, for rebuking, for correcting, for training in righteousness, ¹⁷ so that the man of God may be complete, equipped for every good work.

DAY 9: MEDITATION & MEMORIZATION

QUESTIONS FOR REFLECTION

01

How are the disciplines of meditation and memorization taught by Jesus? How are they discussed in Scripture?

02

How does today's Scripture reading change your understanding of meditation and memorization? How have you seen meditation and memorization modeled in a healthy way? How have you seen them misused or distorted?

Just as you do not analyze the words of someone you love, but accept them as they are said to you, accept the Word of Scripture and ponder it in your heart, as Mary did. That is all. That is meditation.

DIETRICH BONHOEFFER

03

What fruit could come from practicing these disciplines?

04

What could it look like to incorporate the practices of meditation and memorization into your life?

DAY 10

FASTING

The practice of voluntarily laying down an appetite in order to reorient your focus on God.

date   /   /

Isaiah 58:3–7

³ "Why have we fasted, but you have not seen?
We have denied ourselves, but you haven't noticed!"

"Look, you do as you please on the day of your fast,
and oppress all your workers.
⁴ You fast with contention and strife
to strike viciously with your fist.
You cannot fast as you do today,
hoping to make your voice heard on high.
⁵ Will the fast I choose be like this:
A day for a person to deny himself,
to bow his head like a reed,
and to spread out sackcloth and ashes?
Will you call this a fast
and a day acceptable to the LORD?
⁶ Isn't this the fast I choose:
To break the chains of wickedness,
to untie the ropes of the yoke,
to set the oppressed free,
and to tear off every yoke?
⁷ Is it not to share your bread with the hungry,
to bring the poor and homeless into your house,
to clothe the naked when you see him,
and not to ignore your own flesh and blood?"

Luke 4:1–4

¹ Then Jesus left the Jordan, full of the Holy Spirit, and was led by the Spirit in the wilderness ² for forty days to be tempted by the devil. He ate nothing during those days, and when they were over, he was hungry. ³ The devil said to him, "If you are the Son of God, tell this stone to become bread."

⁴ But Jesus answered him, "It is written: Man must not live on bread alone."

Matthew 6:16–18
HOW TO FAST

¹⁶ "Whenever you fast, don't be gloomy like the hypocrites. For they disfigure their faces so that their fasting is obvious to people. Truly I tell you, they have their reward. ¹⁷ But when you fast, put oil on your head and wash your face, ¹⁸ so that your fasting isn't obvious to others but to your Father who is in secret. And your Father who sees in secret will reward you."

Matthew 9:14–17
A QUESTION ABOUT FASTING

¹⁴ Then John's disciples came to him, saying, "Why do we and the Pharisees fast often, but your disciples do not fast?"

¹⁵ Jesus said to them, "Can the wedding guests be sad while the groom is with them? The time will come when the groom will be taken away from them, and then they will fast. ¹⁶ No one patches an old garment with unshrunk cloth, because the patch pulls away from the garment and makes the tear worse. ¹⁷ And no one puts new wine into old wineskins.

NOTES

Otherwise, the skins burst, the wine spills out, and the skins are ruined. No, they put new wine into fresh wineskins, and both are preserved."

John 4:31–38

⁳¹ In the meantime the disciples kept urging him, "Rabbi, eat something."

³² But he said, "I have food to eat that you don't know about."

³³ The disciples said to one another, "Could someone have brought him something to eat?"

³⁴ "My food is to do the will of him who sent me and to finish his work," Jesus told them. ³⁵ "Don't you say, 'There are still four more months, and then comes the harvest'? Listen to what I'm telling you: Open your eyes and look at the fields, because they are ready for harvest. ³⁶ The reaper is already receiving pay and gathering fruit for eternal life, so that the sower and reaper can rejoice together. ³⁷ For in this case the saying is true: 'One sows and another reaps.' ³⁸ I sent you to reap what you didn't labor for; others have labored, and you have benefited from their labor."

John 6:48–51

⁴⁸ "I am the bread of life. ⁴⁹ Your ancestors ate the manna in the wilderness, and they died. ⁵⁰ This is the bread that comes down from heaven so that anyone may eat of it and not die. ⁵¹ I am the living bread that came down from heaven. If anyone eats of this bread he will live forever. The bread that I will give for the life of the world is my flesh."

Revelation 19:6–10

⁶ Then I heard something like the voice of a vast multitude, like the sound of cascading waters, and like the rumbling of loud thunder, saying,

> Hallelujah, because our Lord God, the Almighty, reigns!
> ⁷ Let us be glad, rejoice, and give him glory, because the marriage of the Lamb has come, and his bride has prepared herself.
> ⁸ She was given fine linen to wear, bright and pure.

For the fine linen represents the righteous acts of the saints.

⁹ Then he said to me, "Write: Blessed are those invited to the marriage feast of the Lamb!" He also said to me, "These words of God are true." ¹⁰ Then I fell at his feet to worship him, but he said to me, "Don't do that! I am a fellow servant with you and your brothers and sisters who hold firmly to the testimony of Jesus. Worship God, because the testimony of Jesus is the spirit of prophecy."

DAY 10: FASTING

QUESTIONS FOR REFLECTION

01

How is the discipline of fasting taught by Jesus? How is it discussed in Scripture?

02

How does today's Scripture reading change your understanding of fasting? How have you seen fasting modeled in a healthy way? How have you seen it misused or distorted?

More than any other single discipline, fasting reveals the things that control us.

RICHARD FOSTER

03

What fruit could come from practicing this discipline?

04

What could it look like to incorporate the practice of fasting into your life?

ACTIVE FAITH

Throughout the Gospels, Jesus repeatedly uses action verbs to describe what it means to be His disciple. These instructions help us understand the living, active reality of becoming like Christ.

Disciples of Jesus…

FOLLOW HIM

"If anyone wants to follow after me, let him deny himself, take up his cross, and follow me." MT 16:24

"Follow me…and I will make you fish for people." Immediately they left their nets and followed him. MK 1:17-18

Jesus loved him and said to him, "You lack one thing: Go, sell all you have and give to the poor, and you will have treasure in heaven. Then come, follow me." MK 10:21

After this, Jesus went out and saw a tax collector named Levi sitting at the tax office, and he said to him, "Follow me." LK 5:27

When he saw Jesus passing by, he said, "Look, the Lamb of God." The two disciples heard him say this and followed Jesus. JN 1:36-37

The next day Jesus decided to leave for Galilee. He found Philip and told him, "Follow me." JN 1:43

"My sheep hear my voice, I know them, and they follow me." JN 10:27

ACKNOWLEDGE HIM

"Therefore, everyone who will acknowledge me before others, I will also acknowledge him before my Father in heaven." MT 10:32

"Go home to your own people, and report to them how much the Lord has done for you and how he has had mercy on you." MK 5:19

SEEK HIM

"But seek first the kingdom of God and his righteousness…" MT 6:33

"Whoever does not bear his own cross and come after me cannot be my disciple." LK 14:27

KNOW HIM	OBEY HIM	ABIDE IN HIM
"Many will say to me, 'Lord, Lord, didn't we prophesy in your name, drive out demons in your name, and do many miracles in your name?' Then I will announce to them, 'I never knew you…'" MT 7:22-23	"Therefore, whoever breaks one of the least of these commands and teaches others to do the same will be called least in the kingdom of heaven. But whoever does and teaches these commands will be called great…" MT 5:19	"Remain in me, and I in you. Just as a branch is unable to produce fruit by itself unless it remains on the vine, neither can you unless you remain in me." JN 15:4
"I am the way, the truth, and the life. No one comes to the Father except through me. If you know me, you will also know my Father. From now on you do know him and have seen him." JN 14:6-7	"For whoever does the will of my Father in heaven is my brother and sister and mother." MT 12:50	"May they all be one, as you, Father, are in me and I am in you. May they also be in us…" JN 17:21
	"Why do you call me 'Lord, Lord,' and don't do the things I say?" LK 6:46	
	"Whoever welcomes this little child in my name welcomes me. And whoever welcomes me welcomes him who sent me. For whoever is least among you—this one is great." LK 9:48	
	"If you continue in my word, you really are my disciples." JN 8:31	
	"If anyone loves me, he will keep my word…The one who doesn't love me will not keep my words…" JN 14:23-24	

DAY 11

SABBATH

The weekly practice of abstaining from work and activity to intentionally worship and rest.

date   /   /

Genesis 2:1–3

¹ So the heavens and the earth and everything in them were completed. ² On the seventh day God had completed his work that he had done, and he rested on the seventh day from all his work that he had done. ³ God blessed the seventh day and declared it holy, for on it he rested from all his work of creation.

Exodus 20:8–11

⁸ "Remember the Sabbath day, to keep it holy: ⁹ You are to labor six days and do all your work, ¹⁰ but the seventh day is a Sabbath to the Lord your God. You must not do any work—you, your son or daughter, your male or female servant, your livestock, or the resident alien who is within your city gates. ¹¹ For the Lord made the heavens and the earth, the sea, and everything in them in six days; then he rested on the seventh day. Therefore the Lord blessed the Sabbath day and declared it holy."

Psalm 92
GOD'S LOVE AND FAITHFULNESS

A psalm. A song for the Sabbath day.

¹ It is good to give thanks to the Lord,
to sing praise to your name, Most High,
² to declare your faithful love in the morning
and your faithfulness at night,
³ with a ten-stringed harp
and the music of a lyre.

⁴ For you have made me rejoice, Lord,
by what you have done;
I will shout for joy
because of the works of your hands.
⁵ How magnificent are your works, Lord,
how profound your thoughts!
⁶ A stupid person does not know,
a fool does not understand this:
⁷ though the wicked sprout like grass
and all evildoers flourish,
they will be eternally destroyed.
⁸ But you, Lord, are exalted forever.
⁹ For indeed, Lord, your enemies—
indeed, your enemies will perish;
all evildoers will be scattered.
¹⁰ You have lifted up my horn
like that of a wild ox;
I have been anointed with the finest oil.
¹¹ My eyes look at my enemies;
when evildoers rise against me,
my ears hear them.

¹² The righteous thrive like a palm tree
and grow like a cedar tree in Lebanon.

¹³ Planted in the house of the Lord,
they thrive in the courts of our God.
¹⁴ They will still bear fruit in old age,
healthy and green,
¹⁵ to declare, "The Lord is just;
he is my rock,
and there is no unrighteousness in him."

Isaiah 58:13–14

¹³ "If you keep from desecrating the Sabbath,
from doing whatever you want on my holy day;
if you call the Sabbath a delight,
and the holy day of the Lord honorable;
if you honor it, not going your own ways,
seeking your own pleasure, or talking business;
¹⁴ then you will delight in the Lord,
and I will make you ride over the heights of the land,
and let you enjoy the heritage of your father Jacob."
For the mouth of the Lord has spoken.

Mark 2:23–28
LORD OF THE SABBATH

²³ On the Sabbath he was going through the grainfields, and his disciples began to make their way, picking some heads of grain. ²⁴ The Pharisees said to him, "Look, why are they doing what is not lawful on the Sabbath?"

²⁵ He said to them, "Have you never read what David and those who were with him did when he was in need and hungry — ²⁶ how he entered the house of God in the time of Abiathar the high priest and ate the bread of the Presence —which is not lawful for anyone to eat except the priests —and also gave some to his companions?" ²⁷ Then he told them, "The Sabbath was made for man and not man for the Sabbath. ²⁸ So then, the Son of Man is Lord even of the Sabbath."

Hebrews 4:1–11
THE PROMISED REST

¹ Therefore, since the promise to enter his rest remains, let us beware that none of you be found to have fallen short. ² For we also have received the good news just as they did. But the message they heard did not benefit them, since they were not united with those who heard it in faith. ³ For we who have believed enter the rest, in keeping with what he has said,

So I swore in my anger,
"They will not enter my rest,"

even though his works have been finished since the foundation of the world. ⁴ For somewhere he has spoken about the seventh day in this way: And on the seventh day God rested from all his works. ⁵ Again, in that passage he says, They will never enter my rest. ⁶ Therefore, since it remains for some to enter it, and those who formerly received the good news did not enter because of disobedience, ⁷ he again specifies a certain day—today. He specified this speaking through David after such a long time:

Today, if you hear his voice,
do not harden your hearts.

⁸ For if Joshua had given them rest, God would not have spoken later about another day. ⁹ Therefore, a Sabbath rest remains for God's people.

¹⁰ **For the person who has entered his rest has rested from his own works, just as God did from his.**

¹¹ Let us, then, make every effort to enter that rest, so that no one will fall into the same pattern of disobedience.

DAY 11: SABBATH

QUESTIONS FOR REFLECTION

01

How is the discipline of Sabbath taught by Jesus? How is it discussed in Scripture?

02

How does today's Scripture reading change your understanding of Sabbath? How have you seen Sabbath modeled in a healthy way? How have you seen it misused or distorted?

Sabbath is an act of resistance.
WALTER BRUEGGEMANN

03

What fruit could come from practicing this discipline?

04

What could it look like to incorporate the practice of Sabbath into your life?

DAY 12

LAMENT

DISCIPLINE OF ENGAGEMENT

The practice of bringing grief, complaint, and sorrow to God.

date   /   /

Psalm 71:9–24

⁹ Don't discard me in my old age.
As my strength fails, do not abandon me.
¹⁰ For my enemies talk about me,
and those who spy on me plot together,
¹¹ saying, "God has abandoned him;
chase him and catch him,
for there is no one to rescue him."
¹² God, do not be far from me;
my God, hurry to help me.
¹³ May my adversaries be disgraced and destroyed;
may those who intend to harm me
be covered with disgrace and humiliation.
¹⁴ But I will hope continually
and will praise you more and more.
¹⁵ My mouth will tell about your righteousness
and your salvation all day long,
though I cannot sum them up.
¹⁶ I come because of the mighty acts of the Lord GOD;
I will proclaim your righteousness, yours alone.

¹⁷ God, you have taught me from my youth,
and I still proclaim your wondrous works.
¹⁸ Even while I am old and gray,
God, do not abandon me,
while I proclaim your power
to another generation,
your strength to all who are to come.
¹⁹ Your righteousness reaches the heights, God,
you who have done great things;
God, who is like you?
²⁰ You caused me to experience
many troubles and misfortunes,
but you will revive me again.
You will bring me up again,
even from the depths of the earth.
²¹ You will increase my honor
and comfort me once again.
²² Therefore, I will praise you with a harp
for your faithfulness, my God;
I will sing to you with a lyre,
Holy One of Israel.
²³ My lips will shout for joy
when I sing praise to you
because you have redeemed me.

²⁴ Therefore, my tongue will proclaim
your righteousness all day long,
for those who intend to harm me
will be disgraced and confounded.

Mark 15:33–34

³³ When it was noon, darkness came over the whole land until three in the afternoon. ³⁴ And at three Jesus cried out with a loud voice, *"Eloi, Eloi, lemá sabachtháni?"* which is translated, "My God, my God, why have you abandoned me?"

John 11:1–44
LAZARUS DIES AT BETHANY

¹ Now a man was sick, Lazarus from Bethany, the village of Mary and her sister Martha. ² Mary was the one who anointed the Lord with perfume and wiped his feet with her hair, and it was her brother Lazarus who was sick. ³ So the sisters sent a message to him: "Lord, the one you love is sick."

⁴ When Jesus heard it, he said, "This sickness will not end in death but is for the glory of God, so that the Son of God may be glorified through it." ⁵ Now Jesus loved Martha, her sister, and Lazarus. ⁶ So when he heard that he was sick, he stayed two more days in the place where he was. ⁷ Then after that, he said to the disciples, "Let's go to Judea again."

⁸ "Rabbi," the disciples told him, "just now the Jews tried to stone you, and you're going there again?"

⁹ "Aren't there twelve hours in a day?" Jesus answered. "If anyone walks during the day, he doesn't stumble, because he sees the light of this world. ¹⁰ But if anyone walks during the night, he does stumble, because the light is not in him."

¹¹ He said this, and then he told them, "Our friend Lazarus has fallen asleep, but I'm on my way to wake him up."

¹² Then the disciples said to him, "Lord, if he has fallen asleep, he will get well."

¹³ Jesus, however, was speaking about his death, but they thought he was speaking about natural sleep. ¹⁴ So Jesus then

told them plainly, "Lazarus has died. [15] I'm glad for you that I wasn't there so that you may believe. But let's go to him."

[16] Then Thomas (called "Twin") said to his fellow disciples, "Let's go too so that we may die with him."

THE RESURRECTION AND THE LIFE

[17] When Jesus arrived, he found that Lazarus had already been in the tomb four days. [18] Bethany was near Jerusalem (less than two miles away). [19] Many of the Jews had come to Martha and Mary to comfort them about their brother.

[20] As soon as Martha heard that Jesus was coming, she went to meet him, but Mary remained seated in the house. [21] Then Martha said to Jesus, "Lord, if you had been here, my brother wouldn't have died. [22] Yet even now I know that whatever you ask from God, God will give you."

[23] "Your brother will rise again," Jesus told her.

[24] Martha said to him, "I know that he will rise again in the resurrection at the last day."

[25] Jesus said to her, "I am the resurrection and the life. The one who believes in me, even if he dies, will live. [26] Everyone who lives and believes in me will never die. Do you believe this?"

[27] "Yes, Lord," she told him, "I believe you are the Messiah, the Son of God, who comes into the world."

JESUS SHARES THE SORROW OF DEATH

[28] Having said this, she went back and called her sister Mary, saying in private, "The Teacher is here and is calling for you."

[29] As soon as Mary heard this, she got up quickly and went to him. [30] Jesus had not yet come into the village but was still in the place where Martha had met him. [31] The Jews who were with her in the house consoling her saw that Mary got up quickly and went out. They followed her, supposing that she was going to the tomb to cry there.

[32] As soon as Mary came to where Jesus was and saw him, she fell at his feet and told him, "Lord, if you had been here, my brother wouldn't have died!"

³³ **When Jesus saw her crying, and the Jews who had come with her crying, he was deeply moved in his spirit and troubled.**

³⁴ "Where have you put him?" he asked.

"Lord," they told him, "come and see."

³⁵ Jesus wept.

³⁶ So the Jews said, "See how he loved him!" ³⁷ But some of them said, "Couldn't he who opened the blind man's eyes also have kept this man from dying?"

THE SEVENTH SIGN: RAISING LAZARUS FROM THE DEAD

³⁸ Then Jesus, deeply moved again, came to the tomb. It was a cave, and a stone was lying against it. ³⁹ "Remove the stone," Jesus said.

Martha, the dead man's sister, told him, "Lord, there is already a stench because he has been dead four days."

⁴⁰ Jesus said to her, "Didn't I tell you that if you believed you would see the glory of God?"

⁴¹ So they removed the stone. Then Jesus raised his eyes and said, "Father, I thank you that you heard me. ⁴² I know that you always hear me, but because of the crowd standing here I said this, so that they may believe you sent me." ⁴³ After he said this, he shouted with a loud voice, "Lazarus, come out!" ⁴⁴ The dead man came out bound hand and foot with linen strips and with his face wrapped in a cloth. Jesus said to them, "Unwrap him and let him go."

Romans 12:15
Rejoice with those who rejoice; weep with those who weep.

DAY 12: LAMENT

QUESTIONS FOR REFLECTION

01

How is the discipline of lament taught by Jesus? How is it discussed in Scripture?

02

How does today's Scripture reading change your understanding of lament? How have you seen lament modeled in a healthy way? How have you seen it misused or distorted?

Lament is a cry of belief in a good God.

ANN VOSKAMP

03

What fruit could come from practicing this discipline?

04

What could it look like to incorporate the practice of lament into your life?

| WEEKLY REFLECTION | date / / |

> We recall, in the presence of our God and Father, your work produced by faith, your labor motivated by love, and your endurance inspired by hope in our Lord Jesus Christ.

1 THESSALONIANS 1:3

Reflect on what you've learned this week. What in the reading grabbed your attention? Which practices felt like an opportunity to cultivate the sort of relationship with God your heart longs for?

Choose a discipline you read about in this second week to intentionally practice in the week ahead. Remember, spiritual disciplines are not a means of salvation. They are an invitation to embrace God's presence in new ways and deepen or awaken your relationship with Him. Use the space below to plan how you can incorporate this practice into your coming week.

I WANT TO PRACTICE THE DISCIPLINE OF

I'LL PRACTICE BY

01

02

03

04

I'LL MAKE SPACE TO PRACTICE THIS DISCIPLINE

M	T	W	TH	F	S/SU
am / pm	am / pm	am / pm	am / pm	am / pm	am / pm

Write a short prayer thanking God for your life as His disciple. Ask Him to guide you in your practice as you seek to know and experience Him more.

DAY 13

GRACE DAY

Take this day to catch up on your reading, pray, and rest in the presence of the Lord.

"If anyone serves me, he must follow me."

JOHN 12:26

NOTES | date / /

DAY 14 | # WEEKLY TRUTH

date / /

Scripture is God-breathed and true. When we memorize it, we carry the good news of Jesus with us wherever we go.

During this study, we are memorizing 1 Timothy 4:7b–9. This week, work on committing the last part of verse 8 to memory. To help, say the passage aloud three times in a row, changing the inflection of your voice or the way you emphasize different words and phrases.

> Train yourself in godliness. For the training of the body has limited benefit, but godliness is beneficial in every way, since it holds promise for the present life and also for the life to come. This saying is trustworthy and deserves full acceptance.
>
> — 1 TIMOTHY 4:7b–9

DAY 15

CELEBRATION

The practice of acknowledging and rejoicing in beauty, goodness, and truth.

date   /   /

2 Samuel 6:12–19

¹² It was reported to King David, "The LORD has blessed Obed-edom's family and all that belongs to him because of the ark of God." So David went and had the ark of God brought up from Obed-edom's house to the city of David with rejoicing. ¹³ When those carrying the ark of the LORD advanced six steps, he sacrificed an ox and a fattened calf. ¹⁴ David was dancing with all his might before the LORD wearing a linen ephod. ¹⁵ He and the whole house of Israel were bringing up the ark of the LORD with shouts and the sound of the ram's horn. ¹⁶ As the ark of the LORD was entering the city of David, Saul's daughter Michal looked down from the window and saw King David leaping and dancing before the LORD, and she despised him in her heart.

¹⁷ They brought the ark of the LORD and set it in its place inside the tent David had pitched for it. Then David offered burnt offerings and fellowship offerings in the LORD's presence. ¹⁸ When David had finished offering the burnt offering and the fellowship offerings, he blessed the people in the name of the LORD of Armies. ¹⁹ Then he distributed a loaf of bread, a date cake, and a raisin cake to each one in the entire Israelite community, both men and women. Then all the people went home.

Luke 2:10–11

¹⁰ But the angel said to them, "Don't be afraid, for look, I proclaim to you good news of great joy that will be for all the people: ¹¹ Today in the city of David a Savior was born for you, who is the Messiah, the Lord."

Luke 4:16–21

¹⁶ He came to Nazareth, where he had been brought up. As usual, he entered the synagogue on the Sabbath day and stood up to read. ¹⁷ The scroll of the prophet Isaiah was given to him, and unrolling the scroll, he found the place where it was written:

¹⁸ The Spirit of the Lord is on me,
because he has anointed me
to preach good news to the poor.
He has sent me
to proclaim release to the captives
and recovery of sight to the blind,
to set free the oppressed,
¹⁹ to proclaim the year of the Lord's favor.

²⁰ He then rolled up the scroll, gave it back to the attendant, and sat down. And the eyes of everyone in the synagogue were fixed on him. ²¹ He began by saying to them, "Today as you listen, this Scripture has been fulfilled."

Luke 15:11–32
THE PARABLE OF THE LOST SON

¹¹ He also said, "A man had two sons. ¹² The younger of them said to his father, 'Father, give me the share of the estate I have coming to me.' So he distributed the assets to them. ¹³ Not many days later, the younger son gathered together all he had and traveled to a distant country, where he squandered his estate in foolish living. ¹⁴ After he had spent everything, a severe famine struck that country, and he had nothing.

NOTES

¹⁵ Then he went to work for one of the citizens of that country, who sent him into his fields to feed pigs. ¹⁶ He longed to eat his fill from the pods that the pigs were eating, but no one would give him anything. ¹⁷ When he came to his senses, he said, 'How many of my father's hired workers have more than enough food, and here I am dying of hunger! ¹⁸ I'll get up, go to my father, and say to him, "Father, I have sinned against heaven and in your sight. ¹⁹ I'm no longer worthy to be called your son. Make me like one of your hired workers."' ²⁰ So he got up and went to his father. But while the son was still a long way off, his father saw him and was filled with compassion. He ran, threw his arms around his neck, and kissed him. ²¹ The son said to him, 'Father, I have sinned against heaven and in your sight. I'm no longer worthy to be called your son.'

²² "But the father told his servants, 'Quick! Bring out the best robe and put it on him; put a ring on his finger and sandals on his feet. ²³ Then bring the fattened calf and slaughter it, and let's celebrate with a feast, ²⁴ because this son of mine was dead and is alive again; he was lost and is found!' So they began to celebrate.

²⁵ "Now his older son was in the field; as he came near the house, he heard music and dancing. ²⁶ So he summoned one of the servants, questioning what these things meant. ²⁷ 'Your brother is here,' he told him, 'and your father has slaughtered the fattened calf because he has him back safe and sound.'

²⁸ "Then he became angry and didn't want to go in. So his father came out and pleaded with him. ²⁹ But he replied to his father, 'Look, I have been slaving many years for you, and I have never disobeyed your orders, yet you never gave me a goat so that I could celebrate with my friends. ³⁰ But when this son of yours came, who has devoured your assets with prostitutes, you slaughtered the fattened calf for him.'

³¹ "'Son,' he said to him, 'you are always with me, and everything I have is yours. ³² But we had to celebrate and rejoice, because this brother of yours was dead and is alive again; he was lost and is found.'"

Romans 12:15
Rejoice with those who rejoice; weep with those who weep.

Philippians 4:8
Finally brothers and sisters, whatever is true, whatever is honorable, whatever is just, whatever is pure, whatever is lovely, whatever is commendable—if there is any moral excellence and if there is anything praiseworthy—dwell on these things.

James 1:17
Every good and perfect gift is from above, coming down from the Father of lights, who does not change like shifting shadows.

DAY 15: CELEBRATION

QUESTIONS FOR REFLECTION

01

How is the discipline of celebration taught by Jesus? How is it modeled and discussed in Scripture?

02

How does today's Scripture reading change your understanding of celebration? How have you seen celebration modeled in a healthy way? How have you seen it misused or distorted?

*We dishonor God as much by fearing and avoiding pleasure as
we do by dependence upon it or living for it.*

DALLAS WILLARD

03

What fruit could come from practicing this discipline?

04

What could it look like to incorporate the practice of celebration into your life?

WORSHIP

DAY 16

The practice of responding to the greatness of God with adoration, praise, and gratitude.

date   /   /

Exodus 34:5–8

⁵ The Lord came down in a cloud, stood with him there, and proclaimed his name, "the Lord." ⁶ The Lord passed in front of him and proclaimed:

The Lord—the Lord is a compassionate and gracious God, slow to anger and abounding in faithful love and truth, ⁷ maintaining faithful love to a thousand generations, forgiving iniquity, rebellion, and sin. But he will not leave the guilty unpunished, bringing the consequences of the fathers' iniquity on the children and grandchildren to the third and fourth generation.

⁸ Moses immediately knelt low on the ground and worshiped.

Psalm 29:2

Ascribe to the Lord the glory due his name;
worship the Lord
in the splendor of his holiness.

Matthew 14:24–33

²⁴ Meanwhile, the boat was already some distance from land, battered by the waves, because the wind was against them. ²⁵ Jesus came toward them walking on the sea very early in the morning. ²⁶ When the disciples saw him walking on the sea, they were terrified. "It's a ghost!" they said, and they cried out in fear.

²⁷ Immediately Jesus spoke to them. "Have courage! It is I. Don't be afraid."

²⁸ "Lord, if it's you," Peter answered him, "command me to come to you on the water."

²⁹ He said, "Come."

And climbing out of the boat, Peter started walking on the water and came toward Jesus. ³⁰ But when he saw the strength of the wind, he was afraid, and beginning to sink he cried out, "Lord, save me!"

³¹ Immediately Jesus reached out his hand, caught hold of him, and said to him, "You of little faith, why did you doubt?"

³² When they got into the boat, the wind ceased.

³³ Then those in the boat worshiped him and said, "Truly you are the Son of God."

Luke 19:35–40

³⁵ Then they brought it to Jesus, and after throwing their clothes on the colt, they helped Jesus get on it. ³⁶ As he was going along, they were spreading their clothes on the road.

⁳⁷ Now he came near the path down the Mount of Olives, and the whole crowd of the disciples began to praise God joyfully with a loud voice for all the miracles they had seen:

³⁸ Blessed is the King who comes
in the name of the Lord.
Peace in heaven
and glory in the highest heaven!

³⁹ Some of the Pharisees from the crowd told him, "Teacher, rebuke your disciples."

⁴⁰ He answered, "I tell you, if they were to keep silent, the stones would cry out."

Acts 3:1–10
HEALING OF A LAME MAN

¹ Now Peter and John were going up to the temple for the time of prayer at three in the afternoon. ² A man who was lame from birth was being carried –there. He was placed each day at the temple gate called Beautiful, so that he could beg from those entering the temple. ³ When he saw Peter and John about to enter the temple, he asked for money. ⁴ Peter, along with John, looked straight at him and said, "Look at us." ⁵ So he turned to them, expecting to get something from them. ⁶ But Peter said, "I don't have silver or gold, but what I do have, I give you: In the name of Jesus Christ of Nazareth, get up and walk!" ⁷ Then, taking him by the right hand he raised him up, and at once his feet and ankles became strong. ⁸ So he jumped up and started to walk, and he entered the temple with them—walking, leaping, and praising God. ⁹ All the people saw him walking and praising God, ¹⁰ and they recognized that he was the one who used to sit and beg at the Beautiful Gate of the temple. So they were filled with awe and astonishment at what had happened to him.

Revelation 5:8–14
THE LAMB IS WORTHY

⁸ When he took the scroll, the four living creatures and the twenty-four elders fell down before the Lamb. Each one had a harp and golden bowls filled with incense, which are the prayers of the saints. ⁹ And they sang a new song:

You are worthy to take the scroll
and to open its seals,
because you were slaughtered,
and you purchased people
for God by your blood
from every tribe and language
and people and nation.
¹⁰ You made them a kingdom
and priests to our God,
and they will reign on the earth.

¹¹ Then I looked and heard the voice of many angels around the throne, and also of the living creatures and of the elders. Their number was countless thousands, plus thousands of thousands. ¹² They said with a loud voice,

Worthy is the Lamb who was slaughtered
to receive power and riches
and wisdom and strength
and honor and glory and blessing!

¹³ I heard every creature in heaven, on earth, under the earth, on the sea, and everything in them say,

Blessing and honor and glory and power
be to the one seated on the throne,
and to the Lamb, forever and ever!

¹⁴ The four living creatures said, "Amen," and the elders fell down and worshiped.

DAY 16: WORSHIP

QUESTIONS FOR REFLECTION

01

How is the discipline of worship taught by Jesus? How is it discussed in Scripture?

02

How does today's Scripture reading change your understanding of worship? How have you seen worship modeled in a healthy way? How have you seen it misused or distorted?

The Christian should be an alleluia from head to foot.

ST. AUGUSTINE

03

What fruit could come from practicing this discipline?

04

What could it look like to incorporate the practice of worship into your life?

HYMN

Holy, Holy, Holy

WORDS
Reginald Heber

MUSIC
John B. Dykes; Last stanza setting and choral ending by David T. Clydesdale

DAY 17

CONFESSION

The practice of admitting sin.

date   /   /

Ezra 9:4–9

⁴ Everyone who trembled at the words of the God of Israel gathered around me, because of the unfaithfulness of the exiles, while I sat devastated until the evening offering. ⁵ At the evening offering, I got up from my time of humiliation, with my tunic and robe torn. Then I fell on my knees and spread out my hands to the Lord my God. ⁶ And I said:

My God, I am ashamed and embarrassed to lift my face toward you, my God, because our iniquities are higher than our heads and our guilt is as high as the heavens. ⁷ Our guilt has been terrible from the days of our ancestors until the present. Because of our iniquities we have been handed over, along with our kings and priests, to the surrounding kings, and to the sword, captivity, plundering, and open shame, as it is today. ⁸ But now, for a brief moment, grace has come from the Lord our God to preserve a remnant for us and give us a stake in his holy place. Even in our slavery, God has given us a little relief and light to our eyes. ⁹ Though we are slaves, our God has not abandoned us in our slavery. He has extended grace to us in the presence of the Persian kings, giving us relief, so that we can rebuild the house of our God and repair its ruins, to give us a wall in Judah and Jerusalem.

Psalm 32:1–5
THE JOY OF FORGIVENESS

Of David. A Maskil.

¹ How joyful is the one
whose transgression is forgiven,
whose sin is covered!
² How joyful is a person whom
the Lord does not charge with iniquity
and in whose spirit is no deceit!

³ When I kept silent, my bones became brittle
from my groaning all day long.
⁴ For day and night your hand was heavy on me;
my strength was drained
as in the summer's heat.   *Selah*
⁵ Then I acknowledged my sin to you
and did not conceal my iniquity.
I said, "I will confess my transgressions to the Lord,"
and you forgave the guilt of my sin.   *Selah*

Matthew 5:23–24

²³ "So if you are offering your gift on the altar, and there you remember that your brother or sister has something against you, ²⁴ leave your gift there in front of the altar. First go and be reconciled with your brother or sister, and then come and offer your gift."

NOTES

Colossians 3:12–17
THE CHRISTIAN LIFE

¹² Therefore, as God's chosen ones, holy and dearly loved, put on compassion, kindness, humility, gentleness, and patience, ¹³ bearing with one another and forgiving one another if anyone has a grievance against another.

> Just as the Lord has forgiven you, so you are also to forgive.

¹⁴ Above all, put on love, which is the perfect bond of unity. ¹⁵ And let the peace of Christ, to which you were also called in one body, rule your hearts. And be thankful. ¹⁶ Let the word of Christ dwell richly among you, in all wisdom teaching and admonishing one another through psalms, hymns, and spiritual songs, singing to God with gratitude in your hearts. ¹⁷ And whatever you do, in word or in deed, do everything in the name of the Lord Jesus, giving thanks to God the Father through him.

James 5:16

Therefore, confess your sins to one another and pray for one another, so that you may be healed. The prayer of a righteous person is very powerful in its effect.

1 Peter 2:9

But you are a chosen race, a royal priesthood, a holy nation, a people for his possession, so that you may proclaim the praises of the one who called you out of darkness into his marvelous light.

1 John 1:5–10
FELLOWSHIP WITH GOD

⁵ This is the message we have heard from him and declare to you: God is light, and there is absolutely no darkness in him. ⁶ If we say, "We have fellowship with him," and yet we walk in darkness, we are lying and are not practicing the truth. ⁷ If we walk in the light as he himself is in the light, we have fellowship with one another, and the blood of Jesus his Son cleanses us from all sin. ⁸ If we say, "We have no sin," we are deceiving ourselves, and the truth is not in us. ⁹ If we confess our sins, he is faithful and righteous to forgive us our sins and to cleanse us from all unrighteousness. ¹⁰ If we say, "We have not sinned," we make him a liar, and his word is not in us.

DAY 17: CONFESSION

QUESTIONS FOR REFLECTION

01

How is the discipline of confession taught by Jesus? How is it modeled and discussed in Scripture?

02

How does today's Scripture reading change your understanding of confession? How have you seen confession modeled in a healthy way? How have you seen it misused or distorted?

If there be any of you who by this means cannot quiet his own conscience herein but require further comfort or counsel, let him come to me or to some other minister of God's Word, and open his grief.

THE BOOK OF COMMON PRAYER

03

What fruit could come from practicing this discipline?

04

What could it look like to incorporate the practice of confession into your life?

DAY 18

SUBMISSION

The practice of surrendering to God's will and seeking the goodness and growth of others over our own rights or interests.

date   /   /

Luke 22:39–42
THE PRAYER IN THE GARDEN

³⁹ He went out and made his way as usual to the Mount of Olives, and the disciples followed him. ⁴⁰ When he reached the place, he told them, "Pray that you may not fall into temptation." ⁴¹ Then he withdrew from them about a stone's throw, knelt down, and began to pray, ⁴² "Father, if you are willing, take this cup away from me—nevertheless, not my will, but yours, be done."

2 Corinthians 10:1–6
PAUL'S APOSTOLIC AUTHORITY

¹ Now I, Paul, myself, appeal to you by the meekness and gentleness of Christ—I who am humble among you in person but bold toward you when absent. ² I beg you that when I am present I will not need to be bold with the confidence by which I plan to challenge certain people who think we are living according to the flesh. ³ For although we live in the flesh, we do not wage war according to the flesh, ⁴ since the weapons of our warfare are not of the flesh, but are powerful through God for the demolition of strongholds. We demolish arguments ⁵ and every proud thing that is raised up against the knowledge of God, and we take every thought captive to obey Christ. ⁶ And we are ready to punish any disobedience, once your obedience is complete.

Ephesians 5:15–33
CONSISTENCY IN THE CHRISTIAN LIFE

¹⁵ Pay careful attention, then, to how you walk—not as unwise people but as wise— ¹⁶ making the most of the time, because the days are evil. ¹⁷ So don't be foolish, but understand what the Lord's will is. ¹⁸ And don't get drunk with wine, which leads to reckless living, but be filled by the Spirit: ¹⁹ speaking to one another in psalms, hymns, and spiritual songs, singing and making music with your heart to the Lord, ²⁰ giving thanks always for everything to God the Father in the name of our Lord Jesus Christ, ²¹ submitting to one another in the fear of Christ.

WIVES AND HUSBANDS

²² Wives, submit to your husbands as to the Lord, ²³ because the husband is the head of the wife as Christ is the head of the church. He is the Savior of the body. ²⁴ Now as the church submits to Christ, so also wives are to submit to their husbands in everything. ²⁵ Husbands, love your wives, just as Christ loved the church and gave himself for her ²⁶ to make her holy, cleansing her with the washing of water by the word. ²⁷ He did this to present the church to himself in splendor, without spot or wrinkle or anything like that, but holy and blameless. ²⁸ In the same way, husbands are to love their wives as their own bodies. He who loves his wife loves himself. ²⁹ For no one ever hates his own flesh but provides and cares for it, just as Christ does for the church, ³⁰ since we are members of his body. ³¹ For this reason a man will leave his father and mother and be joined to his wife, and the two will become one flesh. ³² This mystery is profound, but I am talking about

Christ and the church. ³³ To sum up, each one of you is to love his wife as himself, and the wife is to respect her husband.

Ephesians 6:1–9
CHILDREN AND PARENTS

¹ Children, obey your parents in the Lord, because this is right. ² Honor your father and mother, which is the first commandment with a promise, ³ so that it may go well with you and that you may have a long life in the land. ⁴ Fathers, don't stir up anger in your children, but bring them up in the training and instruction of the Lord.

SLAVES AND MASTERS

⁵ Slaves, obey your human masters with fear and trembling, in the sincerity of your heart, as you would Christ. ⁶ Don't work only while being watched, as people-pleasers, but as slaves of Christ, do God's will from your heart. ⁷ Serve with a good attitude, as to the Lord and not to people, ⁸ knowing that whatever good each one does, slave or free, he will receive this back from the Lord. ⁹ And masters, treat your slaves the same way, without threatening them, because you know that both their Master and yours is in heaven, and there is no favoritism with him.

Philippians 2:3–10

³ Do nothing out of selfish ambition or conceit, but in humility consider others as more important than yourselves. ⁴ Everyone should look not to his own interests, but rather to the interests of others.

CHRIST'S HUMILITY AND EXALTATION

⁵ Adopt the same attitude as that of Christ Jesus,

⁶ who, existing in the form of God,
did not consider equality with God
as something to be exploited.
⁷ Instead he emptied himself
by assuming the form of a servant,
taking on the likeness of humanity.
And when he had come as a man,
⁸ he humbled himself by becoming obedient
to the point of death—
even to death on a cross.
⁹ For this reason God highly exalted him
and gave him the name
that is above every name,
¹⁰ so that at the name of Jesus
every knee will bow—
in heaven and on earth
and under the earth.

Hebrews 13:17 NIV

Have confidence in your leaders and submit to their authority, because they keep watch over you as those who must give an account. Do this so that their work will be a joy, not a burden, for that would be of no benefit to you.

DAY 18: SUBMISSION

QUESTIONS FOR REFLECTION

01

How is the discipline of submission taught by Jesus? How is it discussed in Scripture?

02

How does today's Scripture reading change your understanding of submission? How have you seen submission modeled in a healthy way? How have you seen it misused or distorted?

Lord, make me an instrument of Thy peace.

LA CHLOCHETTE

03

What fruit could come from practicing this discipline?

04

What could it look like to incorporate the practice of submission into your life?

DAY 19

GIVING

DISCIPLINE OF ENGAGEMENT

The practice of sacrificially and generously giving of your money, time, and resources to the work of the gospel.

date   /   /

Deuteronomy 14:22–29
A TENTH FOR THE LORD

[22] Each year you are to set aside a tenth of all the produce grown in your fields. [23] You are to eat a tenth of your grain, new wine, and fresh oil, and the firstborn of your herd and flock, in the presence of the LORD your God at the place where he chooses to have his name dwell, so that you will always learn to fear the LORD your God. [24] But if the distance is too great for you to carry it, since the place where the LORD your God chooses to put his name is too far away from you and since the LORD your God has blessed you, [25] then exchange it for silver, take the silver in your hand, and go to the place the LORD your God chooses. [26] You may spend the silver on anything you want: cattle, sheep, goats, wine, beer, or anything you desire. You are to feast there in the presence of the LORD your God and rejoice with your family. [27] Do not neglect the Levite within your city gates, since he has no portion or inheritance among you.

[28] At the end of every three years, bring a tenth of all your produce for that year and store it within your city gates. [29] Then the Levite, who has no portion or inheritance among you, the resident alien, the fatherless, and the widow within your city gates may come, eat, and be satisfied. And the LORD your God will bless you in all the work of your hands that you do.

Psalm 24:1

The earth and everything in it,
the world and its inhabitants,
belong to the LORD.

Matthew 6:1–4
HOW TO GIVE

[1] "Be careful not to practice your righteousness in front of others to be seen by them. Otherwise, you have no reward with your Father in heaven. [2] So whenever you give to the poor, don't sound a trumpet before you, as the hypocrites do in the synagogues and on the streets, to be applauded by people. Truly I tell you, they have their reward. [3] But when you give to the poor, don't let your left hand know what your right hand is doing, [4] so that your giving may be in secret. And your Father who sees in secret will reward you."

Mark 12:41–44
THE WIDOW'S GIFT

[41] Sitting across from the temple treasury, he watched how the crowd dropped money into the treasury. Many rich people were putting in large sums. [42] Then a poor widow came and dropped in two tiny coins worth very little. [43] Summoning his disciples, he said to them, "Truly I tell you, this poor widow has put more into the treasury than all the others. [44] For they all gave out of their surplus, but she out of her poverty has put in everything she had —all she had to live on."

Acts 4:32–37
ALL THINGS IN COMMON

[32] Now the entire group of those who believed were of one heart and mind, and no one claimed that any of his possessions was his own, but instead they held everything in common. [33] With great power the apostles were giving testimony to the resurrection of the Lord Jesus, and great grace was on all of them. [34] For there was not a needy person among them because all those who owned lands or houses sold them, brought the proceeds of what was sold, [35] and laid them at the apostles' feet. This was then distributed to each person as any had need.

[36] Joseph, a Levite from Cyprus by birth, the one the apostles called Barnabas (which is translated Son of Encouragement), [37] sold a field he owned, brought the money, and laid it at the apostles' feet.

2 Corinthians 8:1–15

[1] We want you to know, brothers and sisters, about the grace of God that was given to the churches of Macedonia:

NOTES

²During a severe trial brought about by affliction, their abundant joy and their extreme poverty overflowed in a wealth of generosity on their part. ³I can testify that, according to their ability and even beyond their ability, of their own accord, ⁴they begged us earnestly for the privilege of sharing in the ministry to the saints, ⁵and not just as we had hoped. Instead, they gave themselves first to the Lord and then to us by God's will. ⁶So we urged Titus that just as he had begun, so he should also complete among you this act of grace.

⁷Now as you excel in everything—in faith, speech, knowledge, and in all diligence, and in your love for us—excel also in this act of grace. ⁸I am not saying this as a command. Rather, by means of the diligence of others, I am testing the genuineness of your love. ⁹For you know the grace of our Lord Jesus Christ:

> **Though he was rich, for your sake he became poor, so that by his poverty you might become rich.**

¹⁰And in this matter I am giving advice because it is profitable for you, who began last year not only to do something but also to want to do it. ¹¹Now also finish the task, so that just as there was an eager desire, there may also be a completion, according to what you have. ¹²For if the eagerness is there, the gift is acceptable according to what a person has, not according to what he does not have. ¹³It is not that there should be relief for others and hardship for you, but it is a question of equality. ¹⁴At the present time your surplus is available for their need, so that their abundance may in turn meet your need, in order that there may be equality. ¹⁵As it is written: The person who had much did not have too much, and the person who had little did not have too little.

2 Corinthians 9:6–15

⁶The point is this: The person who sows sparingly will also reap sparingly, and the person who sows generously will also reap generously. ⁷Each person should do as he has decided in his heart—not reluctantly or out of compulsion, since God loves a cheerful giver. ⁸And God is able to make every

grace overflow to you, so that in every way, always having everything you need, you may excel in every good work. ⁹ As it is written:

> He distributed freely;
> he gave to the poor;
> his righteousness endures forever.

¹⁰ Now the one who provides seed for the sower and bread for food will also provide and multiply your seed and increase the harvest of your righteousness. ¹¹ You will be enriched in every way for all generosity, which produces thanksgiving to God through us. ¹² For the ministry of this service is not only supplying the needs of the saints but is also overflowing in many expressions of thanks to God. ¹³ Because of the proof provided by this ministry, they will glorify God for your obedient confession of the gospel of Christ, and for your generosity in sharing with them and with everyone. ¹⁴ And as they pray on your behalf, they will have deep affection for you because of the surpassing grace of God in you. ¹⁵ Thanks be to God for his indescribable gift!

NOTES

DAY 19: GIVING

QUESTIONS FOR REFLECTION

01

How is the discipline of giving taught by Jesus? How is it discussed in Scripture?

02

How does today's Scripture reading change your understanding of giving? How have you seen giving modeled in a healthy way? How have you seen it misused or distorted?

I do not believe one can settle how much we ought to give. I am afraid the only safe rule is to give more than we can spare. In other words, if our expenditure on comforts, luxuries, amusements, etc. is up to the standard common among those with the same income as our own, we are probably giving too little away. If our charities do not at all pinch or hamper us, I should say they are too small.

C. S. LEWIS

03

What fruit could come from practicing this discipline?

04

What could it look like to incorporate the practice of giving into your life?

| WEEKLY REFLECTION | date / / |

For the Spirit God gave us does not make us timid, but gives us power, love and self-discipline.

2 TIMOTHY 1:7 NIV

Reflect on what you've learned this week. What in the reading grabbed your attention? Which practices felt like an opportunity to cultivate the sort of relationship with God your heart longs for?

WEEK 1 2 3 4

Choose a discipline you read about in this third week to intentionally practice in the week ahead. Remember, spiritual disciplines are not a means of salvation. They are an invitation to embrace God's presence in new ways and deepen or awaken your relationship with Him. Use the space below to plan how you can incorporate this practice into your coming week.

I WANT TO PRACTICE THE DISCIPLINE OF

I'LL PRACTICE BY

01
02
03
04

I'LL MAKE SPACE TO PRACTICE THIS DISCIPLINE

M	T	W	TH	F	S/SU
am / pm	am / pm	am / pm	am / pm	am / pm	am / pm

Write a short prayer thanking God for your life as His disciple. Ask Him to guide you in your practice as you seek to know and experience Him more.

DAY 20

GRACE DAY

Take this day to catch up on your reading, pray, and rest in the presence of the Lord.

And let us consider one another in order to provoke love and good works, not neglecting to gather together, as some are in the habit of doing, but encouraging each other, and all the more as you see the day approaching.

HEBREWS 10:24–25

NOTES

date / /

DAY 21 | # WEEKLY TRUTH

date   /   /

Scripture is God-breathed and true. When we memorize it, we carry the good news of Jesus with us wherever we go.

Over the course of this study, we are memorizing 1 Timothy 4:7b–9. This week, add verse 9. Use the space provided to the left to write the passage several times to help you commit it to memory.

> Train yourself in godliness. For the training of the body has limited benefit, but godliness is beneficial in every way, since it holds promise for the present life and also for the life to come. This saying is trustworthy and deserves full acceptance.
>
> 1 TIMOTHY 4:7b–9

DAY 22

SOLITUDE

The practice of abstaining from interactions with others to be alone with God.

date   /   /

Genesis 28:10–22
JACOB AT BETHEL

[10] Jacob left Beer-sheba and went toward Haran. [11] He reached a certain place and spent the night there because the sun had set. He took one of the stones from the place, put it there at his head, and lay down in that place. [12] And he dreamed: A stairway was set on the ground with its top reaching the sky, and God's angels were going up and down on it. [13] The LORD was standing there beside him, saying, "I am the LORD, the God of your father Abraham and the God of Isaac. I will give you and your offspring the land on which you are lying. [14] Your offspring will be like the dust of the earth, and you will spread out toward the west, the east, the north, and the south. All the peoples on earth will be blessed through you and your offspring. [15] Look, I am with you and will watch over you wherever you go. I will bring you back to this land, for I will not leave you until I have done what I have promised you."

[16] When Jacob awoke from his sleep, he said, "Surely the LORD is in this place, and I did not know it." [17] He was afraid and said, "What an awesome place this is! This is none other than the house of God. This is the gate of heaven."

[18] Early in the morning Jacob took the stone that was near his head and set it up as a marker. He poured oil on top of it [19] and named the place Bethel, though previously the city was named Luz. [20] Then Jacob made a vow: "If God will be with me and watch over me during this journey I'm making, if he provides me with food to eat and clothing to wear, [21] and if I return safely to my father's family, then the LORD will be my God. [22] This stone that I have set up as a marker will be God's house, and I will give to you a tenth of all that you give me."

Genesis 32:24–32
JACOB WRESTLES WITH GOD

[24] Jacob was left alone, and a man wrestled with him until daybreak. [25] When the man saw that he could not defeat him, he struck Jacob's hip socket as they wrestled and dislocated his hip. [26] Then he said to Jacob, "Let me go, for it is daybreak."

But Jacob said, "I will not let you go unless you bless me."

[27] "What is your name?" the man asked.

"Jacob," he replied.

[28] "Your name will no longer be Jacob," he said. "It will be Israel because you have struggled with God and with men and have prevailed."

[29] Then Jacob asked him, "Please tell me your name."

But he answered, "Why do you ask my name?" And he blessed him there.

FAITH IN PRACTICE

NOTES

³⁰ Jacob then named the place Peniel, "For I have seen God face to face," he said, "yet my life has been spared." ³¹ The sun shone on him as he passed by Penuel—limping because of his hip. ³² That is why, still today, the Israelites don't eat the thigh muscle that is at the hip socket: because he struck Jacob's hip socket at the thigh muscle.

Matthew 14:6–14, 22–23

⁶ When Herod's birthday celebration came, Herodias's daughter danced before them and pleased Herod. ⁷ So he promised with an oath to give her whatever she asked. ⁸ Prompted by her mother, she answered, "Give me John the Baptist's head here on a platter." ⁹ Although the king regretted it, he commanded that it be granted because of his oaths and his guests. ¹⁰ So he sent orders and had John beheaded in the prison. ¹¹ His head was brought on a platter and given to the girl, who carried it to her mother. ¹² Then his disciples came, removed the corpse, buried it, and went and reported to Jesus.

FEEDING OF THE FIVE THOUSAND

¹³ When Jesus heard about it, he withdrew from there by boat to a remote place to be alone. When the crowds heard this, they followed him on foot from the towns. ¹⁴ When he went ashore, he saw a large crowd, had compassion on them, and healed their sick.

...

²² Immediately he made the disciples get into the boat and go ahead of him to the other side, while he dismissed the crowds. ²³ After dismissing the crowds, he went up on the mountain by himself to pray. Well into the night, he was there alone.

Mark 1:35–39
PREACHING IN GALILEE

³⁵ Very early in the morning, while it was still dark, he got up, went out, and made his way to a deserted place; and there he was praying. ³⁶ Simon and his companions searched for him, ³⁷ and when they found him they said, "Everyone is looking for you."

³⁸ And he said to them, "Let's go on to the neighboring villages so that I may preach there too. This is why I have come."

A MAN CLEANSED

³⁹ He went into all of Galilee, preaching in their synagogues and driving out demons.

John 16:32

"Indeed, an hour is coming, and has come, when each of you will be scattered to his own home, and you will leave me alone. Yet I am not alone, because the Father is with me."

DAY 22: SOLITUDE

QUESTIONS FOR REFLECTION

01

How is the discipline of solitude taught by Jesus? How is it discussed in Scripture?

02

How does today's Scripture reading change your understanding of solitude? How have you seen solitude modeled in a healthy way? How have you seen it misused or distorted?

> *Let him who cannot be alone beware of community, let him who is not in community beware of being alone…each by itself has profound pitfalls and perils. One who wants fellowship without solitude plunges into the void of words and feelings, and the one who seeks solitude without fellowship perishes in the abyss of vanity, self-infatuation, and despair.*
>
> — DIETRICH BONHOEFFER

03

What fruit could come from practicing this discipline?

04

What could it look like to incorporate the practice of solitude into your life?

DAY 23

SILENCE

The practice of being quiet before God.

date   /   /

1 Kings 19:1–13

¹ Ahab told Jezebel everything that Elijah had done and how he had killed all the prophets with the sword. ² So Jezebel sent a messenger to Elijah, saying, "May the gods punish me and do so severely if I don't make your life like the life of one of them by this time tomorrow!"

³ Then Elijah became afraid and immediately ran for his life. When he came to Beer-sheba that belonged to Judah, he left his servant there, ⁴ but he went on a day's journey into the wilderness. He sat down under a broom tree and prayed that he might die. He said, "I have had enough! Lord, take my life, for I'm no better than my ancestors." ⁵ Then he lay down and slept under the broom tree.

Suddenly, an angel touched him. The angel told him, "Get up and eat." ⁶ Then he looked, and there at his head was a loaf of bread baked over hot stones, and a jug of water. So he ate and drank and lay down again.

⁷ Then the angel of the Lord returned for a second time and touched him. He said, "Get up and eat, or the journey will be too much for you." ⁸ So he got up, ate, and drank. Then on the strength from that food, he walked forty days and forty nights to Horeb, the mountain of God. ⁹ He entered a cave there and spent the night.

ELIJAH'S ENCOUNTER WITH THE LORD

Suddenly, the word of the Lord came to him, and he said to him, "What are you doing here, Elijah?"

¹⁰ He replied, "I have been very zealous for the Lord God of Armies, but the Israelites have abandoned your covenant, torn down your altars, and killed your prophets with the sword. I alone am left, and they are looking for me to take my life."

¹¹ Then he said, "Go out and stand on the mountain in the Lord's presence."

At that moment, the Lord passed by. A great and mighty wind was tearing at the mountains and was shattering cliffs before the Lord, but the Lord was not in the wind. After the wind there was an earthquake, but the Lord was not in the earthquake. ¹² After the earthquake there was a fire, but the Lord was not in the fire. And after the fire there was a voice, a soft whisper. ¹³ When Elijah heard it, he wrapped his face in his mantle and went out and stood at the entrance of the cave.

Suddenly, a voice came to him and said, "What are you doing here, Elijah?"

Psalm 37:3–7

³ Trust in the Lord and do what is good;
dwell in the land and live securely.
⁴ Take delight in the Lord,
and he will give you your heart's desires.

NOTES

⁵ Commit your way to the LORD;
trust in him, and he will act,
⁶ making your righteousness shine like the dawn,
your justice like the noonday.

⁷ Be silent before the LORD and wait expectantly for him;
do not be agitated by one who prospers in his way,
by the person who carries out evil plans.

Psalm 131:1–3
A CHILDLIKE SPIRIT

A song of ascents. Of David.

¹ LORD, my heart is not proud;
my eyes are not haughty.
I do not get involved with things
too great or too wondrous for me.

² **Instead, I have calmed and quieted my soul**
like a weaned child with its mother;
my soul is like a weaned child.

³ Israel, put your hope in the LORD,
both now and forever.

Isaiah 30:15
For the Lord GOD, the Holy One of Israel, has said:
"You will be delivered by returning and resting;
your strength will lie in quiet confidence.
But you are not willing."

Habakkuk 2:20
But the LORD is in his holy temple;
let the whole earth
be silent in his presence.

Mark 6:30–33
³⁰ The apostles gathered around Jesus and reported to him all that they had done and taught. ³¹ He said to them, "Come away by yourselves to a remote place and rest for a while." For many people were coming and going, and they did not even have time to eat.

³² So they went away in the boat by themselves to a remote place, ³³ but many saw them leaving and recognized them, and they ran on foot from all the towns and arrived ahead of them.

DAY 23: SILENCE

QUESTIONS FOR REFLECTION

01

How is the discipline of silence taught by Jesus? How is it discussed in Scripture?

02

How does today's Scripture reading change your understanding of silence? How have you seen silence modeled in a healthy way? How have you seen it misused or distorted?

Let us then lay aside our worries and cares, quiet our minds and concentrate upon the reality of God.

AGNES SANFORD

03

What fruit could come from practicing this discipline?

04

What could it look like to incorporate the practice of silence into your life?

DAY 24

SIMPLICITY

The practice of eliminating internal and external distractions in pursuit of a singular focus on God.

date   /   /

Matthew 5:33–37

[33] "Again, you have heard that it was said to our ancestors, You must not break your oath, but you must keep your oaths to the Lord. [34] But I tell you, don't take an oath at all: either by heaven, because it is God's throne; [35] or by the earth, because it is his footstool; or by Jerusalem, because it is the city of the great King. [36] Do not swear by your head, because you cannot make a single hair white or black. [37] But let your 'yes' mean 'yes,' and your 'no' mean 'no.' Anything more than this is from the evil one."

Luke 10:38–42

[38] While they were traveling, he entered a village, and a woman named Martha welcomed him into her home. [39] She had a sister named Mary, who also sat at the Lord's feet and was listening to what he said. [40] But Martha was distracted by her many tasks, and she came up and asked, "Lord, don't you care that my sister has left me to serve alone? So tell her to give me a hand."

[41] The Lord answered her, "Martha, Martha, you are worried and upset about many things, [42] but one thing is necessary. Mary has made the right choice, and it will not be taken away from her."

Luke 12:15–33

[15] He then told them,

"Watch out and be on guard against all greed, because one's life is not in the abundance of his possessions."

[16] Then he told them a parable: "A rich man's land was very productive. [17] He thought to himself, 'What should I do, since I don't have anywhere to store my crops? [18] I will do this,' he said. 'I'll tear down my barns and build bigger ones and store all my grain and my goods there. [19] Then I'll say to myself, "You have many goods stored up for many years. Take it easy; eat, drink, and enjoy yourself."'

[20] "But God said to him, 'You fool! This very night your life is demanded of you. And the things you have prepared—whose will they be?'

[21] "That's how it is with the one who stores up treasure for himself and is not rich toward God."

[22] Then he said to his disciples, "Therefore I tell you, don't worry about your life, what you will eat; or about the body, what you will wear. [23] For life is more than food and the body more than clothing. [24] Consider the ravens: They don't sow or reap; they don't have a storeroom or a barn; yet God feeds

NOTES

them. Aren't you worth much more than the birds? ²⁵ Can any of you add one moment to his life span by worrying? ²⁶ If then you're not able to do even a little thing, why worry about the rest?

²⁷ "Consider how the wildflowers grow: They don't labor or spin thread. Yet I tell you, not even Solomon in all his splendor was adorned like one of these. ²⁸ If that's how God clothes the grass, which is in the field today and is thrown into the furnace tomorrow, how much more will he do for you—you of little faith? ²⁹ Don't strive for what you should eat and what you should drink, and don't be anxious. ³⁰ For the Gentile world eagerly seeks all these things, and your Father knows that you need them.

³¹ "But seek his kingdom, and these things will be provided for you. ³² Don't be afraid, little flock, because your Father delights to give you the kingdom. ³³ Sell your possessions and give to the poor. Make money-bags for yourselves that won't grow old, an inexhaustible treasure in heaven, where no thief comes near and no moth destroys."

1 Timothy 6:9, 17–19
⁹ But those who want to be rich fall into temptation, a trap, and many foolish and harmful desires, which plunge people into ruin and destruction.

…

INSTRUCTIONS TO THE RICH
¹⁷ Instruct those who are rich in the present age not to be arrogant or to set their hope on the uncertainty of wealth, but on God, who richly provides us with all things to enjoy. ¹⁸ Instruct them to do what is good, to be rich in good works, to be generous and willing to share, ¹⁹ storing up treasure for themselves as a good foundation for the coming age, so that they may take hold of what is truly life.

Hebrews 13:5
Keep your life free from the love of money. Be satisfied with what you have, for he himself has said, I will never leave you or abandon you.

James 4:1–2
¹ What is the source of wars and fights among you? Don't they come from your passions that wage war within you? ² You desire and do not have. You murder and covet and cannot obtain. You fight and wage war. You do not have because you do not ask.

DAY 24: SIMPLICITY

QUESTIONS FOR REFLECTION

01

How is the discipline of simplicity taught by Jesus? How is it discussed in Scripture?

02

How does today's Scripture reading change your understanding of simplicity? How have you seen simplicity modeled in a healthy way? How have you seen it misused or distorted?

Father, I want to know Thee, but my cowardly heart fears to give up its toys…please root from my heart all those things I have cherished so long and which have become a very part of my living self, so that Thou mayest enter and dwell there without a rival.

A. W. TOZER

03

What fruit could come from practicing this discipline?

04

What could it look like to incorporate the practice of simplicity into your life?

Spiritual disciplines are a means of actively following Jesus. These practices do not earn us salvation. Rather, our secure relationship with Jesus is what leads to a change in how we live and act. Below is a look at some of what Scripture says about the relationship between our faith and our actions.

SALVATION IS BY FAITH ALONE

GN 15:6
Abram believed the Lord, and he credited it to him as righteousness.

RM 3:28
For we conclude that a person is justified by faith apart from the works of the law.

RM 4:5
But to the one who does not work, but believes on him who justifies the ungodly, his faith is credited for righteousness.

GL 2:16
Because we know that a person is not justified by the works of the law but by faith in Jesus Christ, even we ourselves have believed in Christ Jesus. This was so that we might be justified by faith in Christ and not by the works of the law…

EPH 2:8-9
For you are saved by grace through faith, and this is not from yourselves; it is God's gift—not from works, so that no one can boast.

WORKS ARE AN OUTPOURING OF GENUINE FAITH

MT 5:15-16

"No one lights a lamp and puts it under a basket, but rather on a lampstand, and it gives light for all who are in the house. In the same way, let your light shine before others, so that they may see your good works and give glory to your Father in heaven."

JN 14:12

"Truly I tell you, the one who believes in me will also do the works that I do. And he will do even greater works than these, because I am going to the Father."

1TH 1:3

We recall, in the presence of our God and Father, your work produced by faith, your labor motivated by love, and your endurance inspired by hope in our Lord Jesus Christ.

JMS 2:18

But someone will say, "You have faith, and I have works." Show me your faith without works, and I will show you faith by my works.

JMS 2:22, 26

You see that faith was active together with his works, and by works, faith was made complete...For just as the body without the spirit is dead, so also faith without works is dead.

Our actions are honoring to the Lord and beneficial for us as the people of God when they are the result of our faith. Hebrews 11, sometimes called the Hall of Faith, provides a summary of many figures who actively lived out their faith.

BY FAITH...

ABEL	NOAH	ABRAHAM	ISAAC	JACOB
Offered to God a better sacrifice than Cain did **11:4**	Built an ark to deliver his family **11:7**	When he was called, obeyed and set out for a place that he was going to receive as an inheritance **11:8**	Blessed Jacob and Esau **11:20**	When he was dying, blessed each of the sons of Joseph **11:21**
		Stayed as a foreigner in the land of promise **11:9**		Worshiped, leaning on the top of his staff **11:21**
		When he was tested, offered up Isaac **11:17**		

MOSES	THE ISRAELITES	RAHAB	GIDEON, BARAK, SAMSON, JEPHTHAH, DAVID, SAMUEL, AND THE PROPHETS
Was hidden by his parents 11:23	Crossed the Red Sea as though they were on dry land 11:29	Welcomed the spies in peace 11:31	Conquered kingdoms, administered justice, obtained promises, shut the mouths of lions, quenched the raging of fire, escaped the edge of the sword, gained strength in weakness, became mighty in battle, and put foreign armies to flight 11:32-34
When he had grown up, refused to be called the son of Pharaoh's daughter and chose to suffer with the people of God 11:24-25	The walls of Jericho fell down after being marched around by the Israelites for seven days 11:30		
Left Egypt behind, not being afraid of the king's anger 11:27			
Instituted the Passover and the sprinkling of the blood, so that the destroyer of the firstborn might not touch the Israelites 11:28			

DAY 25

CHASTITY

The practice of refraining from sexual thought and activity.

date   /   /

Psalm 139:13–16

13 For it was you who created my inward parts;
you knit me together in my mother's womb.

14 I will praise you because I have been remarkably and wondrously made.

Your works are wondrous,
and I know this very well.
15 My bones were not hidden from you
when I was made in secret,
when I was formed in the depths of the earth.
16 Your eyes saw me when I was formless;
all my days were written in your book and planned
before a single one of them began.

Proverbs 5:15–19

15 Drink water from your own cistern,
water flowing from your own well.
16 Should your springs flow in the streets,
streams in the public squares?
17 They should be for you alone
and not for you to share with strangers.
18 Let your fountain be blessed,
and take pleasure in the wife of your youth.
19 A loving deer, a graceful doe—
let her breasts always satisfy you;
be lost in her love forever.

Matthew 5:27–30

27 "You have heard that it was said, Do not commit adultery. 28 But I tell you, everyone who looks at a woman lustfully has already committed adultery with her in his heart. 29 If your right eye causes you to sin, gouge it out and throw it away. For it is better that you lose one of the parts of your body than for your whole body to be thrown into hell. 30 And if your right hand causes you to sin, cut it off and throw it away. For it is better that you lose one of the parts of your body than for your whole body to go into hell."

Romans 12:1–2

1 Therefore, brothers and sisters, in view of the mercies of God, I urge you to present your bodies as a living sacrifice, holy and pleasing to God; this is your true worship. 2 Do not be conformed to this age, but be transformed by the renewing of your mind, so that you may discern what is the good, pleasing, and perfect will of God.

1 Corinthians 6:12–20
GLORIFYING GOD IN BODY AND SPIRIT

12 "Everything is permissible for me," but not everything is beneficial. "Everything is permissible for me," but I will not be mastered by anything. 13 "Food is for the stomach and the stomach for food," and God will do away with both of them. However, the body is not for sexual immorality but for the Lord, and the Lord for the body. 14 God raised up the Lord and

NOTES

will also raise us up by his power. ¹⁵ Don't you know that your bodies are a part of Christ's body? So should I take a part of Christ's body and make it part of a prostitute? Absolutely not! ¹⁶ Don't you know that anyone joined to a prostitute is one body with her? For Scripture says, The two will become one flesh. ¹⁷ But anyone joined to the Lord is one spirit with him.

¹⁸ Flee sexual immorality! Every other sin a person commits is outside the body, but the person who is sexually immoral sins against his own body. ¹⁹ Don't you know that your body is a temple of the Holy Spirit who is in you, whom you have from God? You are not your own, ²⁰ for you were bought at a price. So glorify God with your body.

1 Corinthians 7:1–9
PRINCIPLES OF MARRIAGE

¹ Now in response to the matters you wrote about: "It is good for a man not to have sexual relations with a woman." ² But because sexual immorality is so common, each man should have sexual relations with his own wife, and each woman should have sexual relations with her own husband. ³ A husband should fulfill his marital duty to his wife, and likewise a wife to her husband. ⁴ A wife does not have the right over her own body, but her husband does. In the same way, a husband does not have the right over his own body, but his wife does. ⁵ Do not deprive one another—except when you agree for a time, to devote yourselves to prayer. Then come together again; otherwise, Satan may tempt you because of your lack of self-control. ⁶ I say this as a concession, not as a command. ⁷ I wish that all people were as I am. But each has his own gift from God, one person has this gift, another has that.

A WORD TO THE UNMARRIED

⁸ I say to the unmarried and to widows: It is good for them if they remain as I am. ⁹ But if they do not have self-control, they should marry, since it is better to marry than to burn with desire.

1 Thessalonians 4:1–8

¹ Additionally then, brothers and sisters, we ask and encourage you in the Lord Jesus, that as you have received instruction from us on how you should live and please God—as you are doing—do this even more. ² For you know what commands we gave you through the Lord Jesus.

³ For this is God's will, your sanctification: that you keep away from sexual immorality, ⁴ that each of you knows how to control his own body in holiness and honor, ⁵ not with lustful passions, like the Gentiles, who don't know God. ⁶ This means one must not transgress against and take advantage of a brother or sister in this manner, because the Lord is an avenger of all these offenses, as we also previously told and warned you. ⁷ For God has not called us to impurity but to live in holiness. ⁸ Consequently, anyone who rejects this does not reject man, but God, who gives you his Holy Spirit.

DAY 25: CHASTITY

QUESTIONS FOR REFLECTION

01

How is the discipline of chastity taught by Jesus? How is it discussed in Scripture?

02

How does today's Scripture reading change your understanding of chastity? How have you seen chastity modeled in a healthy way? How have you seen it misused or distorted?

Until the will and the affections are brought under the authority of Christ, we have not begun to understand, let alone accept, His Lordship. The Cross, as it enters the love life, will reveal the heart's truth.

ELISABETH ELLIOT

03

What fruit could come from practicing this discipline?

04

What could it look like to incorporate the practice of chastity into your life?

DAY 26

REMEMBRANCE

The practice of intentionally recounting and reflecting on the faithfulness of God.

date   /   /

Deuteronomy 4:1–9, 32–39
CALL TO OBEDIENCE

¹ Now, Israel, listen to the statutes and ordinances I am teaching you to follow, so that you may live, enter, and take possession of the land the LORD, the God of your ancestors, is giving you. ² You must not add anything to what I command you or take anything away from it, so that you may keep the commands of the LORD your God I am giving you. ³ Your eyes have seen what the LORD did at Baal-peor, for the LORD your God destroyed every one of you who followed Baal of Peor. ⁴ But you who have remained faithful to the LORD your God are all alive today. ⁵ Look, I have taught you statutes and ordinances as the LORD my God has commanded me, so that you may follow them in the land you are entering to possess. ⁶ Carefully follow them, for this will show your wisdom and understanding in the eyes of the peoples. When they hear about all these statutes, they will say, "This great nation is indeed a wise and understanding people." ⁷ For what great nation is there that has a god near to it as the LORD our God is to us whenever we call to him? ⁸ And what great nation has righteous statutes and ordinances like this entire law I set before you today?

⁹ Only be on your guard and diligently watch yourselves, so that you don't forget the things your eyes have seen and so that they don't slip from your mind as long as you live. Teach them to your children and your grandchildren.

...

³² Indeed, ask about the earlier days that preceded you, from the day God created mankind on the earth and from one end of the heavens to the other: Has anything like this great event ever happened, or has anything like it been heard of? ³³ Has a people heard God's voice speaking from the fire as you have, and lived? ³⁴ Or has a god attempted to go and take a nation as his own out of another nation, by trials, signs, wonders, and war, by a strong hand and an outstretched arm, by great terrors, as the LORD your God did for you in Egypt before your eyes? ³⁵ You were shown these things so that you would know that the LORD is God; there is no other besides him. ³⁶ He let you hear his voice from heaven to instruct you. He showed you his great fire on earth, and you heard his words from the fire. ³⁷ Because he loved your ancestors, he chose their descendants after them and brought you out of Egypt by his presence and great power, ³⁸ to drive out before you nations greater and stronger than you and to bring you in and give you their land as an inheritance, as is now taking place. ³⁹ Today, recognize and keep in mind that the LORD is God in heaven above and on earth below; there is no other.

Joshua 4
THE MEMORIAL STONES

¹ After the entire nation had finished crossing the Jordan, the LORD spoke to Joshua: ² "Choose twelve men from the people, one man for each tribe, ³ and command them: Take twelve stones from this place in the middle of the Jordan where the priests are standing, carry them with you, and set them down at the place where you spend the night."

⁴ So Joshua summoned the twelve men he had selected from the Israelites, one man for each tribe, ⁵ and said to them, "Go across to the ark of the LORD your God in the middle of the Jordan. Each of you lift a stone onto his shoulder, one for each of the Israelite tribes, ⁶ so that this will be a sign among you. In the future, when your children ask you, 'What do these stones mean to you?' ⁷ you should tell them, 'The water of the Jordan was cut off in front of the ark of the LORD's covenant. When it crossed the Jordan, the Jordan's water was cut off.' Therefore these stones will always be a memorial for the Israelites."

⁸ The Israelites did just as Joshua had commanded them. The twelve men took stones from the middle of the Jordan, one for each of the Israelite tribes, just as the LORD had told Joshua. They carried them to the camp and set them down there. ⁹ Joshua also set up twelve stones in the middle of the Jordan where the priests who carried the ark of the covenant were standing. The stones are still there today.

¹⁰ The priests carrying the ark continued standing in the middle of the Jordan until everything was completed that the LORD had commanded Joshua to tell the people, in keeping with all that Moses had commanded Joshua. The people hurried across, ¹¹ and after everyone had finished crossing, the priests with the ark of the LORD crossed in the

NOTES

sight of the people. ¹² The Reubenites, Gadites, and half the tribe of Manasseh went in battle formation in front of the Israelites, as Moses had instructed them. ¹³ About forty thousand equipped for war crossed to the plains of Jericho in the Lord's presence.

¹⁴ On that day the Lord exalted Joshua in the sight of all Israel, and they revered him throughout his life, as they had revered Moses. ¹⁵ The Lord told Joshua, ¹⁶ "Command the priests who carry the ark of the testimony to come up from the Jordan."

¹⁷ So Joshua commanded the priests, "Come up from the Jordan." ¹⁸ When the priests carrying the ark of the Lord's covenant came up from the middle of the Jordan, and their feet stepped out on solid ground, the water of the Jordan resumed its course, flowing over all the banks as before.

¹⁹ The people came up from the Jordan on the tenth day of the first month, and camped at Gilgal on the eastern limits of Jericho. ²⁰ Then Joshua set up in Gilgal the twelve stones they had taken from the Jordan, ²¹ and he said to the Israelites, "In the future, when your children ask their fathers, 'What is the meaning of these stones?' ²² you should tell your children, 'Israel crossed the Jordan on dry ground.' ²³ For the Lord your God dried up the water of the Jordan before you until you had crossed over, just as the Lord your God did to the Red Sea, which he dried up before us until we had crossed over.

²⁴ This is so that all the peoples of the earth may know that the Lord's hand is strong, and so that you may always fear the Lord your God."

Psalm 143:4–6
⁴ My spirit is weak within me;
my heart is overcome with dismay.

⁵ I remember the days of old;
I meditate on all you have done;
I reflect on the work of your hands.
⁶ I spread out my hands to you;
I am like parched land before you.   *Selah*

Luke 22:14–20
THE FIRST LORD'S SUPPER

¹⁴ When the hour came, he reclined at the table, and the apostles with him. ¹⁵ Then he said to them, "I have fervently desired to eat this Passover with you before I suffer. ¹⁶ For I tell you, I will not eat it again until it is fulfilled in the kingdom of God." ¹⁷ Then he took a cup, and after giving thanks, he said, "Take this and share it among yourselves. ¹⁸ For I tell you, from now on I will not drink of the fruit of the vine until the kingdom of God comes."

¹⁹ And he took bread, gave thanks, broke it, gave it to them, and said, "This is my body, which is given for you. Do this in remembrance of me."

²⁰ In the same way he also took the cup after supper and said, "This cup is the new covenant in my blood, which is poured out for you."

2 Peter 1:12
Therefore I will always remind you about these things, even though you know them and are established in the truth you now have.

DAY 26: REMEMBRANCE

QUESTIONS FOR REFLECTION

01

How is the discipline of remembrance taught by Jesus? How is it discussed in Scripture?

02

How does today's Scripture reading change your understanding of remembrance? How have you seen remembrance modeled in a healthy way? How have you seen it misused or distorted?

> *To remember the past is to see that we are here today by grace, that we have survived as a gift.*
>
> — FREDERICK BUECHNER

03

What fruit could come from practicing this discipline?

04

What could it look like to incorporate the practice of remembrance into your life?

| WEEKLY REFLECTION | date   /   / |

Don't you know that the runners in a stadium all race, but only one receives the prize? Run in such a way to win the prize. Now everyone who competes exercises self-control in everything. They do it to receive a perishable crown, but we an imperishable crown. So I do not run like one who runs aimlessly or box like one beating the air. Instead, I discipline my body and bring it under strict control, so that after preaching to others, I myself will not be disqualified.

1 CORINTHIANS 9:24–27

Think back on your experience over the past four weeks. Use this space to reflect on and respond to your practice of different spiritual disciplines and how your relationship to them has changed.

WEEK 1 2 3 4

WHICH PRACTICES FELT EASILY ACCESSIBLE TO ME?

WHICH PRACTICES SEEMED MORE DAUNTING?

WHICH DISCIPLINE STOOD OUT TO ME MOST?

WHY?

How has studying and practicing spiritual disciplines enriched my relationship with God?

Are there any disciplines I plan to incorporate into my life moving forward? Are there spiritual disciplines I would still like to study or try?

DAY 27

GRACE DAY

Take this day to catch up on your reading, pray, and rest in the presence of the Lord.

Rest in God alone, my soul, for my hope comes from him.

PSALM 62:5

NOTES

date / /

DAY 28 | WEEKLY TRUTH

date   /   /

Scripture is God-breathed and true. When we memorize it, we carry the good news of Jesus with us wherever we go.

Now that you've memorized 1 Timothy 4:7b-9, recite the full passage to a friend. We've left the artwork extra light on the facing page so you can trace the lettering while meditating on these verses.

> Train yourself in godliness. For the training of the body has limited benefit, but godliness is beneficial in every way, since it holds promise for the present life and also for the life to come. This saying is trustworthy and deserves full acceptance.

1 TIMOTHY 4:7b–9

BENEDICTION

"Come to me, all of you who are weary and burdened, and I will give you rest. Take up my yoke and learn from me, because I am lowly and humble in heart, and you will find rest for your souls. For my yoke is easy and my burden is light."

MATTHEW 11:28-30

SPIRITUAL DISCIPLINES HANDBOOK: PRACTICES THAT TRANSFORM US	by Adele Ahlberg Calhoun
THE RUTHLESS ELIMINATION OF HURRY	by John Mark Comer
CELEBRATION OF DISCIPLINE	by Richard J. Foster
SPIRITUAL DISCIPLINES COMPANION	by Jan Johnson
RENOVATION OF THE HEART	by Dallas Willard
THE SPIRIT OF THE DISCIPLINES	by Dallas Willard

CSB BOOK ABBREVIATIONS

OLD TESTAMENT

GN Genesis	**JB** Job	**HAB** Habakkuk	**PHP** Philippians
EX Exodus	**PS** Psalms	**ZPH** Zephaniah	**COL** Colossians
LV Leviticus	**PR** Proverbs	**HG** Haggai	**1TH** 1 Thessalonians
NM Numbers	**EC** Ecclesiastes	**ZCH** Zechariah	**2TH** 2 Thessalonians
DT Deuteronomy	**SG** Song of Solomon	**MAL** Malachi	**1TM** 1 Timothy
JOS Joshua	**IS** Isaiah		**2TM** 2 Timothy
JDG Judges	**JR** Jeremiah	### NEW TESTAMENT	**TI** Titus
RU Ruth	**LM** Lamentations	**MT** Matthew	**PHM** Philemon
1SM 1 Samuel	**EZK** Ezekiel	**MK** Mark	**HEB** Hebrews
2SM 2 Samuel	**DN** Daniel	**LK** Luke	**JMS** James
1KG 1 Kings	**HS** Hosea	**JN** John	**1PT** 1 Peter
2KG 2 Kings	**JL** Joel	**AC** Acts	**2PT** 2 Peter
1CH 1 Chronicles	**AM** Amos	**RM** Romans	**1JN** 1 John
2CH 2 Chronicles	**OB** Obadiah	**1CO** 1 Corinthians	**2JN** 2 John
EZR Ezra	**JNH** Jonah	**2CO** 2 Corinthians	**3JN** 3 John
NEH Nehemiah	**MC** Micah	**GL** Galatians	**JD** Jude
EST Esther	**NAH** Nahum	**EPH** Ephesians	**RV** Revelation

BIBLIOGRAPHY

Bonhoeffer, Dietrich. *Life Together*. New York: Harper & Row, 1954.

Bonhoeffer, Dietrich. *The Way to Freedom*. Edited by Edwin Hanton Robertson. New York: Harper & Row, 1966.

Brueggemann, Walter. *Sabbath as Resistance*, 1st ed. Louisville: Westminster John Knox Press, 2014.

Buechner, Frederick. *A Room Called Remember*. New York: Harper & Row, 1984.

Calhoun, Adele Ahlberg. *Spiritual Disciplines Handbook*. Revised and Expanded ed. Downers Grove: InterVarsity Press, 2015.

Dillard, Annie. *The Writing Life*. New York: HarperCollins, 1989.

Elliot, Elisabeth. *Passion and Purity*. Grand Rapids: Baker Publishing Group, 1984.

Foster, Richard J. *Celebration of Discipline,* 4th ed. San Francisco: HarperOne, 2018.

Foster, Richard J., and Emilie Griffin. *Spiritual Classics*. San Francisco: Renovaré, 2000.

Foster, Richard J. "Spiritual Disciplines: A Practical Strategy." *Renovaré*. https://renovare.org/about/ideas/spiritual-disciplines

Hendricks, Howard G., and William D. Hendricks. *Living by the Book*. Chicago: Moody Publishers, 1991.

Johnson, Jan. *Spiritual Disciplines Companion*. Downers Grove: InterVarsity Press, 2009.

King, Martin Luther, Jr. "The Drum Major Instinct." Sermon, Ebenezer Baptist Church, Atlanta, February 4, 1968.

Lewis, C. S. *Mere Christianity.* New York: HarperOne, 2001.

Mother Teresa. *A Simple Path*. New York: Ballantine Books, 1995.

Nouwen, Henri J. M. *The Inner Voice of Love*. New York: Doubleday, 1998.

Sanford, Agnes. *The Healing Light*. Eastford: Martino Fine Books, 2013.

"The Peace Prayer." *La Clochette*, December 1912.

Tozer, A. W. *The Pursuit of God*. Harrisburg: Christian Publications, Inc., 1984.

Voskamp, Ann. *One Thousand Gifts*. Grand Rapids: Zondervan, 2010.

Willard, Dallas. *Renovation of the Heart*. Colorado Springs: NavPress, 2002.

Willard, Dallas. *The Spirit of the Disciplines*. New York: HarperCollins, 1988.

 SHE READS TRUTH | BIBLE

Inspired by the She Reads Truth mission of "Women in the Word of God every day," the *She Reads Truth Bible* is thoughtfully and artfully designed to highlight the beauty, goodness, and truth found in Scripture.

FEATURES

- Custom reading plans to help you navigate your time in the Word
- Thoughtful devotionals throughout each book of the Bible
- Maps, charts, and timelines to provide context and Scripture connections
- 66 hand-lettered key verses to aid in Scripture memorization

USE CODE SRTB15 FOR
15% OFF YOUR NEW
SHE READS TRUTH BIBLE!

SHOPSHEREADSTRUTH.COM

FOR THE RECORD

WHERE DID I STUDY?

o HOME
o OFFICE
o COFFEE SHOP
o CHURCH
o A FRIEND'S HOUSE
o OTHER:

WHAT WAS I LISTENING TO?

ARTIST:

SONG:

PLAYLIST:

WHEN DID I STUDY?

MORNING
AFTERNOON
NIGHT

HOW DID I FIND DELIGHT IN GOD'S WORD?

WHAT WAS HAPPENING IN MY LIFE?

WHAT WAS HAPPENING IN THE WORLD?

| MONTH | DAY | YEAR |

END DATE